A Road

Marian L. Mayfield

> *"Stand at the crossroads and look;*
>
> *ask for the ancient paths,*
>
> *ask where the good way is, and walk in it,*
>
> *and you will find rest for your souls."*

~Jeremiah 6:16~

Copyright@2011

Marian L.Mayfield

ISBN-13:

978-1461129417

ISBN-10: 1461129419

Contents

Part I: **Exploring The Spirit**

The Same Yesterday, Tomorrow And Forever

Part II: **The Journey Begins**

Wisdom Of The Ages

Lessons From The Seasons

The Wheel Of The Year

Tree Of Life

Spiritual Meaning Of Various Trees

Part III: **_Coming To Know The Goddess_**

Five Principles Of Intimate Prayer

Part IV : **_Symbols That Define Faith_**

A Look Back In Time

Appalachian Granny Magick

Part V : **_Spiritual Housecleaning_**

Creating Sacred Space, Archangels

Introduction

The purpose of this book is to enlighten others in the blended path of Christianity along with pagan roots. We all search for our own views of what the truth is. The fact being the truth, is in the eyes of the beholder. Through meditation and prayer we all can become more aware of our Creator.

The truth we seek is not out there but within ourselves. There all the time waiting to be explored. It was instilled within us before we were thought of, planted like a seed, waiting to be refreshed with water, longing for the warmth of insight to be embraced, to grow into something each individual can define as themselves.

Sometimes the answers lie within the lessons we see everyday. Nature itself is our teacher. The winds blow and though we cannot see them, doesn't mean they are not present. If we listen we can hear that still small voice. If we seek we shall find. It is also true when we look at the divine creation and how without balance would cease to exist. The earth rotates just so on it's axis, the moon pulls in the waves, the sun warms the earth and gives it light keeping it just so to keep life flowing.

The wheel of life turns in perfect rotation, the seasons come and then pass by. In spring there is rebirth everywhere. New buds of life spring forth from the branches of the trees. We too go through these changes we continue to grow, even threw our storms. For it is our storms that teach us how to be stronger. Through our winters we are still and reflect, and then we too have our own spring of newness. We are reborn threw the lessons of our winters, and our springs.

I dedicate this book to all seekers of wisdom. Whatever your beliefs, I hope this work sheds light on your spirit. With an open mind and heart, I pray you come to a deeper understanding, gather insight into your spiritual life.

As an Eclectic I tend to learn from all belief systems, not claiming just one. My belief is everyone's path is their own. No one should pass judgment on what is within your heart. There are many out in the world that would pose the question," How can one practice a blended spirituality?"

I believe the answers lie within your own heart, waiting to be discovered. The answers to many questions people have are already within they have been there all the time, like a fire waiting to be rekindled.

I dedicate this book to all the wise teachers I have had to pleasure of crossing paths with in my life. Some have gone from my life now, but will always be remembered through the stories and lessons they shared. Their words resonate within me even now, waiting to be put down on paper so they might live once again.

To my beautiful children, who teach me something new each day. I remember to go with a child-like heart, seeing things and people for not only for what they are but for what they stand for. To look beyond the human eyes of sight and see the heart.~ *In Perfect Love And Perfect Trust*~

Exploring The Spirit

Have you ever been curious of what Spirit is made up of? Spirit is the intangible, unseen force with us all that drives us to seek to understand the Divine in a more intimate way.

To live being lead by spirit is to see the works of the Creator in a way most overlook, to hear the voice upon the winds of change that urge us onward in our journey.

It is what animates us, crossing the bridge between body and soul. In Christianity the Holy Spirit is the one sent to us to give us enlightenment on issues in life.

In paganism the pentacle aligns spirit as the top of the star, because we should always let spirit be the thriving force in our lives.

To combine the two beliefs is not unheard of, it all resides within the individual to seek their own path, to create their own reality of how they become closer to the Divine and also begin to realize that the Divine also resides within.

The definition of pagan, has long been misunderstood and misinterpreted.. *paganus* a Latin word simply means country dweller,civilian *pagus:* from a country rural district.

Almost as the words country hick,or redneck are used today.It simply meant those people over there that seem different than us.

It all started at the rise of Christianity.When the word started to spread throughout the Roman empire,and in other places.The Romans used this conation to describe the last of those who became follower of the different sects of Christianity.During the Crusades,it was thrown around to describe Muslims,Gentiles and people of the West.

The word was used as a divider of sorts to show the difference in "us" and "them".Someone not like them used to describe others of any religion,who held strong to their old ways of belief.

The Crusades opened a new door,into a vast hunt for those in their minds should accept their ideals of Christ or death.This was so unlike the Jesus they claimed to follow.

Jesus Christ loved all people,being unjudgemental of anyone.In all cost violence was never His answer.

This can be described in the scriptures,Jesus was well known to be from Nazareth.The place was considered the lowest of places.Nothing good ever seemed to come out of this place.Jesus Himself probably suffered these labels of sort in his place of coming up.He also was friends with tax-collectors,prostitutes and thieves even adulterers...he ate with them and even some of His apostles were of such background.

So to explain this definition,in greater detail...it was meant to be a division.That was not necessarily a good thing.It took unity out of the equation and fear arose of anyone who didn't see the Divine just like the Romans.

Spirit is within all things.This is the definition of Animism.

There is nothing that is just an object,everything is an extension of the Divine and contains spirit.

This is a core belief of all pagans.All things are connected in one form or another.The seed becomes the plant that grows and gives forth to life.

Animals feed off these and we them.All things are born and then die giving way to something born anew.

The universe is a master plan of the Creator and moves in perfect harmony.

The tides are governed by the moons pull.The earth is cooled and heated in complete balance of temperature.Revolving on its axis in perfect time.The cosmic dust of space and the earth gave way to the first humans.

We were all created out of the dust itself.The breath of life was given to us threw the Creator threw oxygen and life giving air.I believe Breath contains one's spirit.

To this we are too extensions of the Divine.Not only in a physical state but in a spiritual state.In Genesis 1:26 it states "Let us make human beings in our image, in our likeness, so that they may rule over the fish in the sea and the birds in the sky, over the livestock and all the wild animals, and over all the creatures that move along the ground."

Though we rule over,we still consider these things sacred as they are part of creation.I also want to point out in this scripture the word "Us"this explains how God is One and Many..Omnipresent.Of both male and female .To propose there could actually be a God and Goddess.

Many scriptures touch on this.In Song Of Solomon the Goddess is described as wisdom.

In Revelation the twelfth chapter,a woman is mentioned clothed with the sun and the moon under her feet,she wore a crown of twelve stars.She is known as the Queen of Heaven.

Native Americans consider the sky their father and the earth their mother. Why is it so unspeakable in some churches to acknowledge the feminine?

To consider both aspects is to truly know yourself..for we all are born with both qualities. In utero we all start as female. To have both within a human yet be one person a whole describes further how God can be many yet One.

Christianity also has similarities with the pagan way, Let's consider the Wiccan Law in correlation to the scriptures:

The Wiccan Rede (short version)

Bide the Wiccan Laws ye must

In perfect love and perfect trust.

Eight words the Wiccan Rede fulfill,

An ye harm none, do what ye will.

Lest in thy self-defense it be,

Ever mind the rule of three.

Follow this in mind and heart,

And Merry Meet and Merry Part!

KJV Bible:Therefore all things whatsoever ye would that men should do to you, do ye even so to them: for this is the law and the prophets.Matt7:12

In the fourth stanza of the Wiccan Rede,it clearly states and harm ye none,do as ye will.

This explains that you may do as you will,that it doesn't bring harm to other beings.The next stanza discusses self defense..this would be in the case that one does harm towards you.

The Rule of Three,is the effect the universe would give back to those doing harm,such as a karma effect.

What you put out towards others or yourself be it good or bad would come back to you..such as a boomerang thrown would eventually come back to where it came.

If we as humans treat others according to how we ourselves would wish to be treated,with love respect and kindness then expect the same in return.This process would bring peace.People are to reach for the highest potential in how they respond to society as a whole.

Code of Chivalry

- Chivalry is a high code of honor which is of most ancient Pagan origin, and must be lived by all who follow the Old ways.

- It must be understood that thoughts and intent put forth on this plane will wax strong in other planes, and return... bringing into creation, on this world, that which had been sent forth. Thus, you should exercise discipline, for "as ye do plant, so shall ye harvest".

- It is only by preparing our minds to be as Gods that we can ultimately attain godhead.

- Above all else, you must be true to yourself.

- A witches' word must have the validity of a signed and witnessed oath. Thus, give thy word sparingly, but adhere to it like iron.

- Refrain from speaking ill of others, for not all truths of the matter may be known.

- Pass not unverified words about another, for hearsay is, in large part, a thing of falsehoods.

- Be honest with others, and let them know that honesty is also expected of them.

- The heat of the moment plays havoc with the truth. To keep your head is a virtue.

- Contemplate always the consequences of your actions upon others. Strive not to harm.

- Different covens may well have diverse views on love between members and with others. When a coven, clan, or grove is visited or joined, you should always find out their practices and abide by them, or leave.

- Dignity, a gracious manner, and a good humor are much to be admired.

- As a witch, you have power, and your powers wax strongly as wisdom increases. Therefore, exercise discretion in their use.

- Courage and honor endure forever. Their echoes remain when the mountains have crumbled to dust.

- Pledge friendship and fealty to those who warrant it. Strengthen others of this path and they will strengthen you.

- You must not reveal the secrets of another witch or another coven. Others have labored long and hard for them, and cherish them as a treasure.

- Though there may be differences between those of the Old Ways, those who are once-born must see nothing and must hear nothing.

- Those who follow the mysteries should be above reproach in the eyes of the world.

- The laws of the land should be obeyed whenever possible and within reason, for the most part they have been chosen with wisdom.

- Have pride in yourself and seek perfection in mind and body. For the Lady asks "How cast thou honor another unless thou give honor to thyself first?"

- Those who seek the mysteries should consider themselves as select of the Gods, for it is they who lead the race of humankind to the highest of thrones and beyond the stars.

This information was taken from 'Magical Rites from the Crystal Well' by Ed Fitch.

In the third stanza of the code of chivalry,it speaks of preparing our minds as that of the Divine.In Matthew 22:37 it states:Jesus said unto him, Thou shalt love the Lord thy God with all thy heart, and with all thy soul, and with all thy mind.

 This scripture is saying we should love with our whole heart,mind,and spirit.I will remind you that in Genesis 7:22,Job

12:10,Psalm 33:6 all discuss the breath of the Creator.

To become out of the breath of the Divine is to be in the image not only as one would think a physical image,as we are all both male and female.

As a spiritual image,the same as the breath of life in which was breathed into the first of all creation.To become like that of the Divine,is to have the mind of the Divine,the heart and spirit also.

Now let's explore the second threw ninth stanzas,this is talking of the saying as above so below.We should strive to be as the Divine in all that we do,including being truthful,not judging others,being honorable and also being true to ourselves.

The Same Yesterday, Tomorrow And Forever

Is it so unheard of to assume Jesus was on the scene for centuries, even before the rise of Christianity? I would like to propose my theory on this subject.

Jesus has many faces to the human psyche but yet is still the same Deity. After all in the primal days when there were writings and cave paintings on the walls, of early mankind, One might have seen pictures of a horned man..because the hunt of animals was crucial to survive.

Early ones might have even made this a God of sorts. In their minds this was the God of the hunt. This is why today we refer to The Horned god as the God of Wicca.

It is not a reference to Satan, or the devil etc. I can assure you that no pagan I have ever met has anything to do with the devil, nor do they even acknowledge the existence.

In truth the devil of the Bible was written in by the Catholic Church to become the parallel of the deity Pan who was a mythological figure often spoke of by the pagans.

The church also borrowed many of the now celebrated holidays from the pagans such as

Easter,Christmas etc..I will discuss this in later chapters.

The Horned God is represented in carved icons of the Neolithic era,found in Europe (c.4300 B.C.)Human-like in appearance these carving represented metaphors of the dying and rebirth of vegetation.

He was known as The Lord Of The Forest.With Stag horns that quite possibly represented the hunter-gathers plight to seek food.

In Egypt hieroglyphs depictions of Horus,who was the embodiment of divine goodness, wisdom, truth and purity...This was the greatest hero that ever lived in the mind of man -- not in the flesh -- the only hero to whom the miracles were natural because he was not human." Gerald Massey, author of "The Natural Genesis,"

Horus was also believed to be born of the virgin Isis,died and resurrected,also raised the dead.In later times he was affiliated with the newborn sun.

Isis was given the titles of Our Lady,Queen Of Heaven,Mother of God,and Immaculate Virgin.

The Egyptian god Osiris,accompanied the dead to their resurrection,was called "the soul that lives again""the first born of unformed matter"and "the lord of life for all eternity"

The title Good Shepherd was shard by Horus, Apollo, and Mercury. Jesus was also said to be The Good Shepard

Dionysus is pictured in inscriptions as riding a donkey on the way to his death.

The pre-Christian god Mithras - called the Son of God and the Light of the World - was born on December 25, died, was buried in a rock tomb, and then resurrected in three days.

By the way, December 25 was also the birthday of Osiris, Adonis, and Dionysus.

Within the many traditions in which Dionysus is associated with wine, grapes and alcohol, there is a claim that he performed a miracle of turning water into wine, at a wedding.

"According to myth, the miracle of turning water into wine took place for the first time at the marriage of Dionysus and Ariadne. This same miracle is attributed to Jesus at the wedding feast in Cana." - The Jesus Mysteries.

Adonis is one of the many pagan deities that some scholars and writers characterize as a pre-Christian god who, like Jesus, was born of a virgin, died and was resurrected. Often summarized as an annual "life-death-rebirth" vegetation god, meaning that he was associated with the agricultural cycle, during which plants die in the winter and revive in the spring.

The Adonis tradition is often said to have originated with the Babylonian myth of Tammuz, by way of Syria, before being imported into Greek mythology. It also is claimed that the Etruscan legend of Attunis and the German myth of Baldr were copied from the Adonis tradition.

I often still depict Jesus as the wise,gentle teacher.Druid-like.The following is a definition of a druid:

> The Druids were the wise ones, the educated class of the Celts. They were the lawyers, doctors, teachers, storytellers, and other professional of that culture. They were more than just clergy.

As Christianity increased in influence, the role of Bard and Storyteller became split from religion. Traditions lived on in legend and secular practice. The Druids did not write their traditions in their own language. These were carried in song and poetry from generation to generation.

There is strong evidence that seems to ring clear that Jesus' story has been and will always be threw the ages.Even by a different identity.Identities came up with by mankind.After all how do you define Spirit?How can you measure the magnificent Deity of the Lord in just one name,one face.Spirit is like that,the wind is unseen but yet it is still there.

To explain the Lord is impossible,not one person can..to know Him is more of an emotion of heart,a breath of sweet life that gives abundance,the smell of a rose..that one can't describe in just words.In that matter not just one word.Past lives well maybe,and why not?It is said He is the same yesterday,today and forever.Like the circle never ending..with no beginning.

"For nearly a hundred years, we have known that the material world is an illusion. Everything that seems solid - a rock, a tree, your body - is actually 99.999% empty space."

Deepak Chopra

{Omnipresent [ˌɒmnɪˈprɛzənt]

(esp of a deity) present in all places at the same time

omnipresence n Collins English Dictionary – Complete and Unabridged © HarperCollins Publishers 1991, 1994, 1998, 2000, 2003}

—Synonyms

Omnipresent, ubiquitous refer to the quality of being everywhere. Omnipresent emphasizes in a lofty or dignified way the power, usually divine, of being present everywhere at the same time, as though all-enveloping: Divine law is omnipresent.

I Suppose this is why they refer to Him as Omnipresent!

"Within the last century several books have been published to supplement the meager descriptions in the Gospels of Jesus and His ministry. In some instances these narratives claim to be founded upon early manuscripts recently discovered; in others, upon direct spiritual revelation.

Some of these writings are highly plausible, while others are incredible. There are persistent rumors that Jesus visited and studied in both Greece and India, and that a coin struck in His honor in India during the first century has been discovered.

Early Christian records are known to exist in Tibet, and the monks of a Buddhist monastery in Ceylon still preserve a record which indicates that Jesus sojourned with them and became conversant with their philosophy.

It is by no means improbable that Jesus Himself originally propounded as allegories the cosmic activities which were later confused with His own life.

That the Χριστός, Christos, represents the solar power reverenced by every nation of antiquity cannot be controverted. If Jesus revealed the nature and purpose of this solar power under the name and personality of Christos, thereby giving to this abstract power the attributes of a god-man, He but followed a precedent set by all previous World-Teachers.

This god-man, thus endowed with all the qualities of Deity, signifies the latent divinity in every man. Mortal man achieves deification only through at-one-moment with this divine Self. Union with the immortal Self constitutes immortality, and he who finds his true Self is therefore "saved."

This Christos, or divine man in man, is man's real hope of salvation--the living Mediator between abstract Deity and mortal humankind.

As Atys, Adonis, Bacchus, and Orpheus in all likelihood were originally illumined men who later were confused with the symbolic personages whom they created as personifications of this divine power, so Jesus has been confused with the Christos, or god-man, whose wonders He preached. Since the Christos was the god-man imprisoned in every creature, it was the first duty of the initiate to liberate, or "resurrect, " this Eternal One within himself.

He who attained reunion with his Christos was consequently termed a Christian, or Christened, man.

One of the most profound doctrines of the pagan philosophers concerned the Universal Savior-God who lifted the souls of regenerated men to heaven through His own nature.

This concept was unquestionably the inspiration for the words attributed to Jesus: "I am the way, the truth, and the life: no man cometh unto the Father but by me."

In an effort to make a single person out of Jesus and His Christos, Christian writers have patched together a doctrine which must be resolved back into its original constituents if the true meaning of Christianity is to be rediscovered.

In the Gospel narratives the Christos represents the perfect man who, having passed through the various stages of the "World Mystery" symbolized by the thirty-three years, ascends to the heaven sphere where he is reunited with his Eternal Father. The story of Jesus as now preserved is--like the Masonic story of Hiram Abiff--part of a secret initiatory ritualism belonging to the early Christian and pagan Mysteries.

During the centuries just prior to the Christian Era, the secrets of the pagan Mysteries had gradually fallen into the hands of the profane. To the student of comparative religion it is evident that these secrets, gathered by a small group of faithful philosophers and mystics, were reclothed in new symbolical garments and thus preserved for several centuries under the name of Mystic Christianity.

It is generally supposed that the Essences were the custodians of this knowledge and also the initiators and educators of Jesus. If so, Jesus was undoubtedly initiated in the same temple of Melchizedek where Pythagoras had studied six centuries before.

The Essences--the most prominent of the early Syrian sects--were an order of pious men and women who lived lives of asceticism, spending their days in simple labor and their evenings in prayer. Josephus, the great Jewish historian, speaks of them in the highest terms.

"They teach the immortality of the soul," he says, "and esteem that the rewards of righteousness are to be earnestly striven for." In another place he adds, "Yet is their course of life better than that of other men and they entirely addict themselves to husbandry. " The name Essences is supposed to be derived from an ancient Syrian word meaning "physician," and these kindly folk are believed to have held as their purpose of existence the healing of the sick in mind, soul, and body.

According to Edouard Schuré, they had two principal communities, or centers, one in Egypt on the banks of Lake Maoris, the other in Palestine at Engaddi, near the Dead Sea.

Some authorities trace the Essenes back to the schools of Samuel the Prophet, but most agree on either an Egyptian or Oriental origin. Their methods of prayer, meditation, and fasting were not unlike those of the holy men of the Far East." From(Ashmole's Order of the Garter.)

Although early Christianity shows every evidence of Oriental influence, this is a subject the modern church declines to discuss.

If it is ever established beyond question that Jesus was an initiate of the pagan Greek or Asiatic Mysteries, the effect upon the more conservative members of the Christian faith is likely to be cataclysmic.

If Jesus was God incarnate, as the solemn councils of the church discovered, why is He referred to in the New Testament as "called of God an high prim after the order of Melchizedek"?

The words "after the order" make Jesus one of a line or order of which there must have been others of equal or even superior dignity. If the "Melchizedeks" were the divine or priestly rulers of the nations of the earth before the inauguration of the system of temporal rulers, then the statements attributed to St. Paul would indicate that Jesus either was one of these "philosophic elect" or was attempting to reestablish their system of government.

It will be remembered that Melchizedek also performed the same ceremony of the drinking of wine and the breaking of bread as did Jesus at the Last Supper.

The word "Magi" is merely the Latin equivalent of "Druid." In many Celtic records the word Magi is used instead of Druid.

After its creation, the story of Jesus was transplanted from Britain, where it was invented, to Galilee and Judea. This was done so that Christianity would not appear to be conspicuously Druidic in nature.

To conceive Christianity in Britain was one thing; to birth it there was another. The Atonists realized their warped religion was based on ancient Amenism and Druidism.

They knew their Jesus (their Iesus or Yeshua) was based on the Druidic Iesa or Aesar, and that nearly every educated person in the world would know it also.

Their difficulty concerned how to come up with a believable king of light sufficiently appealing to the world's many pagan nations.

Their employees, such as St. Paul (Josephus Piso), were, therefore, allowed to plunder the archive of the pagans.

They were instructed to draw from the canon of stellar gnosis and from the ancient solar theologies of Egypt, Chaldea, and Ireland.

The archetypal elements would, like ingredients, simply be tossed about and rearranged and, most importantly, the territory of the new god-man would be re-situated to suit the plan."

— Michael Tsarion; The Irish Origins of Civilization, Volume 1

" Not only is Jesus often referred to as the Fisher of Men, but as John P. Lundy writes: "The word Fish is an abbreviation of this whole title, Jesus Christ, Son of God, Savior, and Cross; or as St. Augustine expresses it, 'If you join together the initial letters of the five Greek words, Ἰησοῦς Χριστος Θεου Υἰοσ Σωτήρ, which mean Jesus Christ, Son of God, Savior, they will make ΙΧΘΥΣ,

Fish, in which word Christ is mystically understood, because He was able to live in the abyss of this mortality as in the depth of waters, that is, without sin.'" (Monumental Christianity.) Many Christians observe Friday, which is sacred to the Virgin (Venus), upon which day they shall eat fish and not meat.

The sign of the fish was one of the earliest symbols of Christianity; and when drawn upon the sand, it informed one Christian that another of the same faith was near."

— (Manly P. Hall; The Secret Teachings of all Ages)

Summary

In this chapter I have went to lengths to describe the similarities that are within the Old Ways and Christianity.

I have also touched on the subject of Jesus being Omnipresent,in definition and by way of the gods of mythology that have such similar resemblances to Jesus that it cannot be ignored.Including his life,death and resurrection.

I would like to also point out that in the Bible the people mistook Jesus' for Elijah reincarnated:

Matthew 16:14 (Today's New International Version)

14 They replied, "Some say John the Baptist; others say Elijah; and still others, Jeremiah or one of the prophets."

Jesus also taught in parables,using ways of Nature for most of his teachings.Paganism being a nature centered religion this is very significant.

We as pagans honor the earth and consider all things sacred and from the divine,to be acknowledged as an extension of the Creator.It is by no surprise that when the crowds asked Jesus why it was that he taught in parables,or riddles he answered...Matthew 13:13

This is why I speak to them in parables: "Though seeing, they do not see; though hearing, they do not hear or understand.

The Parables of the Mustard Seed and the Yeast

31 He told them another parable: "The kingdom of heaven is like a mustard seed, which a man took and planted in his field. 32 Though it is the smallest of all seeds, yet when it grows, it is the largest of garden plants and becomes a tree, so that the birds come and perch in its branches."

I believe here Jesus was speaking of the fact that simplicity describes the kingdom,yet not to be taken for granted.People of the day were more inclined to hear the message with use of parable..

It made simple truths easy to understand even though in reality the message was such it could not be explained to the average person..that is if they had not reached enlightenment.

To say they had not adapted the mind and divinity of Christ.

The kingdom is after all also within every individual,only on a personal basis does one come to know the Divine in his or her own way.They are totally responsible for self.

If Christ lives within us all,how do we reflect Him to others?Do we come off as judgmental to others beliefs,critical and demeaning or do we show the fruits of the spirit,and show love(God is Love)biblical,(Love is The Law)A.Crowley Thelema-both viewpoiunts point this message out clearly.

Romans 13:8

[Love Fulfills the Law] Let no debt remain outstanding, except the continuing debt to love one another, for whoever loves others has fulfilled the law.

Romans 13:7-9 (in Context) Romans 13 (Whole Chapter)

Romans 13:8

John 13:35

By this everyone will know that you are my disciples, if you love one another.

The Journey Begins

Closing my eyes, to hear the soft breeze singing songs of recognition outside my window.The owl's lonely hoot seems to be calling to me,I drift on and on into a peaceful summer's night sleep.

Crickets call as to a lover,the rain.I hear the gentle drops start to fall from the heavens washing over me like a mist of cleansing.I am rejuvenated once again,dreams of what could be settle in my mind once again as the usually will,compelling me to move on,to be strong,not give up.

As the wind sings my name threw the night,I am comforted.The sun and the moon constantly seek each other,as star crossed lovers over time and space,sometimes once to eclipse,then centuries of the same artful,dance,that revolves their child Earth.

Her light from the father..pulls the tide..growing her children as a mother's love does..the father's fire reflects on her once again,the oceans move,no longer are their children's waters stagnant,Flowing with life.

Winds blow from all directions,as guards,as angels,as the elements,who have been and will always be to..move the dust,clearing her mountains,healing her tides,calling the names,the sacred names of their children.

"GO,ye are the ones who will teach your children and their children.The mystery that is not!"For once the infinite mysteries are revealed,they find the knew them all along,awake they are,aware,threw new eyes they see..with neither color nor grey.

For they know..once their children feel the warmth of the father,a new seed grows out of time,a seed ,quickening in the hearts of those who understand.

The path I walk,holds no fear,the road ahead beakons me onward.The burden is light,I am carried as the wind carried the mighty hawk across the sky..to just glide.

I am rooted as the tree beside the streams of glorious colors,all colors of stone and time,My roots grow deeper still within my mother..my branches lift to my father,ever attempting to be in between the worlds,that are vivid and those of reality,ever seeking balance of the two.

The rains fall from the Father across the field and new growth begins,time turns the wheel,also within myself.

In the spring new abundance,new life,summer has it's growth too,fall there is harvest and winter all dies to be renewed.

The ancient ones and those before smile down on me,letting me know yes,we are still here as a lighthouse guiding you onward my child.

We send our animals as messengers as angels unaware,to teach lessons that only can be seen by eyes that see,can only be heard by those ears without restraint.

As the deer,I come to you my child,the grown stag,Price of the Forest.Sewing gentle comfort as you go along your path.I am quick,I am alert,I see by night with eyes of faith.

My mother embrases me in her arms,as the rain over dry fields,as the earth I lie upon to be returned to once again.Spirit as the ocean waters,the Sun,calls the drops of rain back once again.

On the gentle breeze,I smell the scents of roses knowing,my mother is here.It's all going to be ok sugar,keep going.

{Stanza From The Gospel Of Peace}

"Peace I bring to thee, my children,

The Sevenfold Peace

Of the Earthly Mother

And the Heavenly Father.

Peace I bring to thy body,

Guided by the Angel of Power; Peace I bring to thy heart,

Guided by the Angel of Love; Peace I bring
to thy mind,

Guided by the Angel of Wisdom. Through
the Angels of

Power, Love and Wisdom,

Thou shalt travel the Seven Paths

Of the Infinite Garden,

And thy body, thy heart and thy mind

Shall join in Oneness

In the Sacred Flight to the Heavenly Sea of
Peace.

In the depths of darkness,even though
invisible I feel You there...Your whispers of

ancient secrets fill my ears, my heart with gratitude,hope for tomorrow.

As the morning Sun rises I am reminded all is new again,You never give up on us..The dawning of the new day is the dawning of opportunity to strengthen ourselves,to Know ourselves...

What is spoken in the night,within our spirit;You tell us shout it on the mountaintops...

When we are in the valleys too-You stand in un condition,in a hooded robe of glory,(Teacher),wisdom is Yours and ours too for the taking..

You show yourself in many ways..Even with antlers of the gentle deer.that is strong,quick and just it's struggle to survive the questions of the dark,You are Gentleness.You are there in the sites we see in nature the Butterfly that starts out without wings,in the process becomes free..

The corn that withers in the fall..to bring newness next season..

The wheel of the season as it turns-I see you there..No ending no beginning..In winter there is sleep to the earth,But still the Moon shines bright,on the fallen snow sparkling like a diamond..

In spring new buds on the trees..this is how I see you..

the autumn, summer are in between --It is ALL lessons for us..on how we grow,how we die and are reborn..how there is Nothing that ever really ends.

Spirit is like the wind,,It passes by us..although we cannot see it.It is still there.The winds of change come,we age we learn -we continue to seek.

When we seek we find..and sometimes what we have been seeking has been within all along.Still we are quickened to continue on..keep on seeking

I can see You in a newborn child,in the peace that is- when we finally die to this life..

I feel you as I raise my arms..winds rush in behind me..lifting me as though my spirit were going to soar away like the mighty eagle,

I ask and I am given insight..You appear as the graceful Hawk..always watching over me...

You remind me Who I am..that I am.That I was put here for a purpose.

You are Love..that is You..

When I close my eyes I can hear your whispers on the wind..That you have always been..the same today,tomorrow and yesterday..The same yet different in the concept in the human mind...

Society still fights who is wrong or right..I can hear You in your still small voice.There

is no right or wrong..division is chaos and
You are Not Chaos..You are Wisdom,You
are Peace,You can be one and
many,Omnipresent..There is nothing
Impossible.

You remind us we are Goddess..because we
are all born of division of sexes yet when we
come together we become one.

So this is my love story to You..Within my
heart I am reminded in the power of
simplicity,You appear as the mighty Oak
that leads me on a journey in my dreams..

I spiral to see You as the water..That fills
me.You remind me..If you pour out your
entire chalice of water on others..You
yourself suffer..Drink..And Never thirst.

I see you in the brilliance of Fire ..you burn
with transformations..you change a once
material thing into ashes..it reminds me-I too
am only that..Dust.

But as the smoke rises so does my spirit
with yours dancing threw the flames..

In my journey-You remind me..One day
though you are looking at this looking glass

darkly..not seeing the true Me You will one day..Put like this when we come face to face..We see Ourselves.

Our eyes are windows of the past and pasts..

In the shadow of your wings -I am comforted..I sleep with the knowing that ALL is well

Wisdom Of The Ages

Wisdom is in where you find it. Sometimes hiding in plain sight. So be content to keep searching ,for without the search the veil remains when you find it; cherish it like a deep treasure.

SOME treasures should only be shared with those who are wise enough to know that they are truly not. To find wisdom in the simplicity of Self worth dignity pride in yourself. it is hidden in plain sight your treasure is who you see staring back at you in the mirror. IT IS YOU:)

People tend to strive to understand so many things in so little time,which is a good thing.When someone comes to the final conclusion they have learned all they can about life,it's mysteries and it's realities they tend to become arrogant.

Things tend to change in this person they become numb to the fact of learning more,opening up their minds,or their hearts to anything new..HERE starts the corruption of the light of this in-material thing we call wisdom,To those who become set in their ways the light,or the shimmer of the pearl of wisdom dies out,dims in effect to self-righteous ideas that others are wrong for their beliefs......Lets take Galileo for instance,or any of the great minds of the past that set in motion their own ideas,their own thoughts..which were choked out by the society that should embrace them.

Here begats ignorance..see to me wisdom doesn't take alot of thought process it is an inconceivable, indestructible,notion,a rare pearl that few find,and that only some see..People find enlightenment,ideas,knowledge in the strangest of places..does this make them any less..NO I think not.

You can find wisdom in a single shaft of grain,the dead seeds fall again to produce new wheat for the next year,the wheat shaft nourishes the seeds until they fall..these could easily be new ideas,now thoughts for the future,the old must die for a new thing to take shape to grow if you will.

Wisdom can be found in books yes,but the deepest wisdom lies within all of us, in the smallest lessons we learn from the mundane,smallest things.The things around us,the stillness of reflection of winter,when new ideas hibernate within our very spirit to be reborn in the warmth of the sun of spring,

Seeing events of the past,going forward,knowing that even though times have been hard..we learned from them just the same.

This is wisdom she tells us,learn from the past,go on,the old seeds of regret,remorse,will soon fall away and die and new birth ALWAYS happens..so in essense wisdom never fails us,unless of course we fail her......In that I mean becoming numb,no longer allowing new growth becoming stagnant in the waters we call our life journey,

Are you going to remain in the pond of those who believe they have learned everything they need to know and nothing else matters,there is nothing else,or like ancients of the past such as Galileo..make a splash out into the ocean of many voices allowed to speak as they will flowing with the other currents,not stifled by the dams of those who tell you-you can't.

The currents come from many a place but yet become the ocean,they represent each other,work with each other,not repress,destroy or become overbearing..this is not wisdom but folly.....such as waves that crash around a single man on a boat..The voice of wisdom and love speaks and the waves become peaceful again..urging EACH of us..use your own voice.Be who you are,no matter the outcome..because in the end.....Is it not coming to the grips of the ultimate wisdom which is to love,without restraint,without regret,without guilt..This is Real love..the kind that you do not have to force.

As the wind sings my name through the night,I am comforted.The sun and the moon constantly seek each other,as star crossed lovers over time and space,sometimes once to eclipse,then centuries of the same artful,dance,that revolves their child Earth.

Her light from the father..pulls the tide..growing her children as a mother's love does..the father's fire reflects on her once again,the oceans move,no longer are their children's waters stagnant,Flowing with life.

Winds blow from all directions,as guards,as angels,as the elements,who have been and will always be to..move the dust,clearing her mountains,healing her tides,calling the names,the sacred names of their children."

GO,ye are the ones who will teach your children and their children.The mystery that is not!"For once the infinite mysteries are revealed,they find the knew them all along,awake they are,aware,through new eyes they see..with neither color nor grey.

For they know..once their children feel the warmth of the father,a new seed grows out of time,a seed ,quickening in the hearts of those who understand.

  I believe in the glimmer of hope behind a wish~

Unhindered strength of courage in one's heart

Never ending love within one's spirit...

Endless wisdom in simplicity...

The voice of LOVE in each drop of spring rain..

A knot of FAITH tied to bind.

Joy comes in time; washing away our pain.

With the morning sun,that reminds-

There is POWER in Prayer,upon waking and before sleep...

POWER in LOVE

POWER in Wishes of Peace

OUR faith is not shaken by the storm we see..

If we believe,as we wish.

At times I feel like I have lost my way,unsure what the future holds.I hang on th blind faith,take a leap and keep going.This still small voice that we all have should be a compass when the roads of life appear to be at a dead end,detour or even stressing wrong way.I stay on my path,knowing what I know,remembering where I have been,unsure of where I am going but standing on faith.

Faith is believing in the unseen,believing in things that seem impossible..but are if you believe in yourself.

Some people may not understand may not accept me but that is their loss I am who I am.Strong-willed unwilling to give up or give in,I am my own worst critic when times seem the darkest,there is a light leading me on.

I may have lost myself,lost my understanding of the (why)things play out as they do.This is when the detour sign comes to mind;there is ALWAYS a detour,doesn't matter if you look hard enough there are several possibilities to EVERY situation.

The dead end sign comes to mind.Symbolically this sign could mean various things.The Spirit is telling you,wait,be patient,stop trying to handle things on your own.Wait and pray.Back up and watch things work themselves threw.It may not be in our time but will be on time.

In reality there is not a dead-end or a wrong way,these (symbolic road signs)lie because you see in England you would not necessarily be going the WRONG Way..it's all on the way we look at it.What seems wrong to many is right.

The dead end..is really not -beyond that sign there is always an off road that can be taken to get to your destination.

So wherever this road is taking me ..I will know when I get there.I hang on to that compass that always points me in the right direction.Symbolically I call this a compass of faith.The needle continues to point me,and I follow.

I have came to the conclusion that everyone's(roads)may not appear to be the same,In the end however we all reach our destination.The same destination.If we follow our own hearts..~

Lessons From The Seasons
===

 As the autumn leaves fall,I am reminded of things I need to let go of,to make a better harvest of the spirit for next year.It is out with the old and in with the new.

Nature too,is about death,resurrection and rebirth.We all struggle threw this life,think we want things,only to find out after all it wasn't meant for us to have,new agenda,new desires,new beginnings..surface around this time of the year..as the trees put on the last show of fall colors,brilliance of color,the winds blow them to the ground to keep the grounds warm,knowing winter will be coming soon.

Winter is a time of reflection,as animals hibernate,so do we as humans kindle things in our hearts and memories in front of a fire on a cold winter's day.

Newness is coming,a new start,a clean slate as the snow glistens under the moonlight.Reflecting of things that once were and will be,reflecting on the warmth of the spark of love within our hearts.melting the ice of self-doubt.We too become whiter than snow,new strength within our bones.Springtime comes and the wheel still turns,new buds grow from the trees as within our own hearts too.To lay down the old,feels so empowering.After all,when we look into the mirror,we see not only a physical reflection..on second look what others see within us.No one is responsible for our actions but us.

When we look into a mirror as a glass darkly,then face to face..sometimes peering back is what we could be.The flame still burns threw a long winter's night.Now is the time when there is perfect balance between the night and day.A new year,new beginnings.

As the leaves begin to turn I am reminded of the many colors,experiences,that my life has had the joy of knowing.Both good and bad.Now the trees are almost bare,the winds blow the leaves to the ground,to cover the new growth of grass beneath them with a blanket of protection.

The leaves beneath me remind me of times in my life I wanted to give up,Times in my life I became bold and followed through.

Times I cried,laughed,rejoiced in the simple things in life.The leaves that fall are the pages of my life.Maybe the end of a chapter,in due time new again budding forth new life as spring I know is on it's way

.After the long cold winter,A time a reflection,I reflect upon myself.The ice turns cold promises un kept,holding them in still form until warmth of the sun comes once again.Life is truly about hope,love,pain,regret,being,knowing,wisdom,chance,birth,life,death,rebirth..

It is within us it is within our surroundings..weaving lessons only noticed by some.Lessons of going on,weathering the storm,understanding that the sad times are of a temporary nature,painful yet temporary none the less..they times fall from the tree in experience of lessons learned,become something good,the leaves(our hopes,fears,regrets and joys)Mix together to blanket the earth.

Something new always arises if we wait if we believe if we have hope.

There are some trees evergreen,staying green year round,remind us..persevere :nothing ever really dies,nothing is ever really lost.I think we tend to loose sight of the fact.Life is about experience.

Though pages of our life fall as the autumn leaves,we are wiser none the less,more equipped to battle life,better than the day before.Ready to live another day unshaken by the wind.

A new sagely boldness arises in me,as I look at the everlasting life of a simple ever green tree,see the magick the lessons that are whispered to me.If only to notice simple things,to see the new life of spring,the budding of the rose,that the autumn leaves kept warm in the winter of stillness.To bloom once again.

How insane it is to constantly be fighting,within our own psyche.As a people we are battling ourselves constantly with this or that,who we are,who we aspire to be,fear sometimes drives us onward..fear of the unknown..of tomorrow and what will come.

Fear is necessary in small doses..for survival instincts to kick in..it gets us fired up on making sure our future generations are well-took care of,better adjusted to life,

In the depths of our being..we all know this is crucial..Just as the animal kingdom,raise our young,hope to be the hunter not the hunted so to speak.

In today's society..money,success,a name make a person(who) they are..a net worth.OK,let's flip this picture.

Consider those who came before us that came from nothing,presidents,leaders,mothers,even someone who stood up for their rights as human to be treated as an equal.It took the notion of conquering fears,to get these people where they saw themselves.

The following is my theory on the balance of two opposites,such as positivity and negativity.Both have to be present to keep things in line:

There were three crosses..The middle cross,is where my Lord..was in one of his many forms,threw the times and ages of man.His mission was clear and drawn out already.

The two other crosses were of the thieves,one was compassionate to Jesus and told the other,This man hasn't done anything.The other thief was silent..I do not necessarily think that the silence was of no remorse..I believe it may have been out of enlightenment of what had just been revealed to the other thief.

Basically,the three crosses the middle was the balancer of the scales that measure..humans spiritual side.

Just like the story in Native tradition,the two wolves fighting within a man/woman..the one you feed wins.There has to be a balance of darkness,it soaks up,Light reflects like a prism..without both the other could not existist in a balance.Note I am not speaking of good and evil here.I am speaking of a bigger message that Is with out the middle equaling the two= there out both would cancel each other out. +=-,

It takes the balance of the scales ,and the positive and negative aspects of our psyche to balance ,what is most light as a feather..is just simplicity and looking at things..through a different kind of perception.

When you put on rose-colored,or 3-d glasses so to speak.

 It seems, the more we (seek) through life we find,this proves true in all things spiritual,personal and otherwise.

I believe it is a good thing to question everything,to weigh it all out.I've been analytical most of my years,It has proves to be beneficial, in the outcome. No matter,what you are questioning,digging deeper into the mystery we call life.

I suppose, I have now came to the point in my path.Where I am just satisfied and content to be.

Through soul-searching,prayer,meditation and listening to the things revealed.I have this conclusion.

We seek and seek and break down everything,But what if in the end what you have broke down so to speak,just becomes again a void,By void..I am saying not desolation..but we realize everything broken down,starts to have no form at all.

In a dream ,I dreamt of those who have came before me..My totems/spirit guides were also there as usual.I was given a key..

to all the questions and answers I asked,and sought after..throughout the beginning of my childhood even.

I was pointed to the door,by the Lord and Lady and was told "Now is the time..to know" Opening the door,I saw a mirror of my own reflection!

It's basically a simple concept,I am the one searching for something intangible,that I Have always had the answers staring me in the face,just wasn't listening!

The key to what you seek,you have all your life,sometimes it takes experience,time,pain,joy and some growing to do.

The answer I received,was simple yet so profound.Seek after yourself,eventually you find your inward psych and let go off all fears,bewilderment,and constant searching. Your left with a simple truth,Just KNOW,and go along for the ride so to speak!The conclusion we receive truth,confidence,peace,and a satisfied spirit.

The answer is"Don't take yourself so seriously,You have the answers deep within,No matter in what light you find your true path,It was kindling within your deepest being all along,You have the key,always have,But I find not all doors are locked to us(spiritually speaking)We just assume they are.The wisdom we search for day to day,is already there,just need to open the door to see your own reflection.

It is the responsibility of us all,to accept we can not change others,only what is within our own spirit...sometimes need to be examined.What we find is our own reflection,telling us,from the deities..It's up to you..to teach my people!

This is not the beginning of my story,just a taste.Going to sleep last night.I was asked,What do you seek child?Why do you worry?What makes you happy.

my answer,my children..I want them to be taken care of,I feel I fall short at times,I want them to be happy.

I wish for the end of the book so to speak,to know what will be,to create alternate endings,happy endings.I want to be a light,be the salt..to others,to stop the pain,dry the tears of society,right the wrongs..

Then I was asked,once again What makes..Marian.YOU happy?

My answer was clear as if a fog had been lifted,the key to what I want is comfort.Trust rushed in..more of a confident trust..I just knew my kids will be ok,one day when I'm 80..I will see the whys.

I was challenged this..Without words.BREATH!Just breath and I literally took a deep breath as in being born,or dying..it was..PURE peace.Breath we - rush,worry,and we sometimes..literally forget..take some deep breaths and just go!

Just BE!Air..oxygen,here is the literal breath of life..our first gift,we often take for granted.

We are as drops of rain that fall from the heavens,down to the earth into the oceans,the sun condensends,the fires and heat(within our spirit)gently force the raindrop, back again to form of air,back to where it came once again..only to fall again as clouds form..it's a cycle,a circle,never ending..no beginning.

If you force a butterfly out of it's cocoon crysilis ,too soon..it dies.

Nature knows,time promotes growth.Transformation happens in small doses at a time.Once broken out of the cocoon the butterfly has conquered,flight is it's gift.

Why do we daily,not give our heart the same reverence?Only a heart with wings can fly.Gentleness is the best defense,Patience..

As for the end of the book,I so want to know..I already do.It has already been written out,I realize the pages turn to slowly at times for me,Slow it down,breath,relax..

Just as a wild mustang,I let myself run and run seeking freedom,running from..but It amazes me how better it is to run To...A slower pace,to just know..All is Well..Almost as if this mustang ran off a cliff..but has grown her wings,Hope drives you on..a single leap and you finally realize..you can fly,float let the winds carry you on.

The key here..Faith!

Stars fall, we wish. With a childlike heart for things thus unseen in the mundane world..but yet here is the magic of belief.

Time takes it's toll on us all,we become wiser,loose our youth,Realization sets in and we realize..that like the stars we once wished on,like the daffodils we once blew with wishes on the wind have came and past,some wishes came true some still unresolved.

The sun still rises the moon still lights our path,we walk in blind faith,wondering still wishing in our hearts to know the final outcome,which we know in within ourselves.

Within our very being and spirit,is the falling star,is the seed of the daffoldill..though we might not see where the journey of life is leading us,the magick lies within us,has never left us..though time turns the pages of our lives our age,lessons are learned,our hearts learn to go on ,possibly never to mend..but grow stronger like a diamond in the rough,once cleaned ,put threw the fire..

A diamond shines through different faucets of light,prism effect..All our simple wishes all the dreams on the wind..fade away one day..but we do go on..because wherever there is a seed planted,whomever we have made a difference in someone else's life,we go on like a pebble dropped into a stream the ripple effect goes on,wishes are still made,hearts fall in love and are broken,time turns the page rebuilding the damage.

It all comes down to balance..the balance of our minds,heart,will..I think when our time is done here on earth in this life..some way we go on,and receive the things we (wished)for in life..filled and satisfied..the true magick is within you..it is simplicity,the sight of a butterfly drifting on the wind,the beat of a heart of a young girl in love,the sound of the ocean,the smell of the rain coming after a long hot summer day..

Within our

souls...

lie the answers to the questions

we have yet to even ask ourselves,

hidden so deep beneath the surface

yet very close to our beating hearts,

waiting impatiently to emerge

when the timing is just right."

"Within our souls...

lives the memories of a lifetime

we have yet to even experience,

hidden just below the surface

while our anxious hearts

wait even more impatiently

for love to finally free our spirit

The Wheel Of The Year

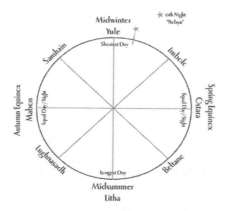

In the Pagan tradition, the wheel of the year is celebrated as a time to reap and harvest spiritual knowledge and also abundances acquired throughout the year. There are eight Sabbats. These are usually always held in a sacred place considered holy ground in the place of choosing. These are considered, to honor the manifestation of the Divine.

There are cycles throughout life, the seasons and the years. The practices are observed and grow deeper in meaning throughout the coming years.

Offering a deep meditative prayerful state..for what has come and gone. To learn the lessons that once posed questions. The

Sabbats are a time of reflection,wishes for the coming year and practices of seeing the blessings given in life.

The change of the seasons symbolically is also a change in our growth spiritually and otherwise.This is a sacred time of healing.We are working with mother earth not against her to learn the deep lessons that Jesus also taught between the lines of His parables.

The four great Sabbats:Samhain,Imbolc,Beltane and Lammas.These honor the Celtic seasonal cycle as it was observed in Western Europe.

The four"cross quarter"Sabbats revolve around the solar cycles.These include:

- Winter Solstice,also known as Yule.

- Summer Solstice,also known as Midsummer.

- Spring Equinox

- Fall Equinox

This is the basis of the "wheel of the year"That is always turning,always promoting growth in nature and within ourselves.Creating harmony and balance.

We can also find this deeper meaning of the turning of the wheel in scriptures:

Ecclesiastes 3

New Living Translation (NLT)

A Time for Everything

1 For everything there is a season,

    a time for every activity under heaven.

2 A time to be born and a time to die.

    A time to plant and a time to harvest.

3 A time to kill and a time to heal.

    A time to tear down and a time to build up.

4 A time to cry and a time to laugh.

    A time to grieve and a time to dance.

5 A time to scatter stones and a time to gather stones.

    A time to embrace and a time to turn away.

6 A time to search and a time to quit searching.

    A time to keep and a time to throw away.

7 A time to tear and a time to mend.

A time to be quiet and a time to speak.

8 A time to love and a time to hate.

A time for war and a time for peace.

9 What do people really get for all their hard work? 10 I have seen the burden God has placed on us all. 11 Yet God has made everything beautiful for its own time.

He has planted eternity in the human heart, but even so, people cannot see the whole scope of God's work from beginning to end. 12 So I concluded there is nothing better than to be happy and enjoy ourselves as long as we can. 13 And people should eat and drink and enjoy the fruits of their labor, for these are gifts from God.

Genesis 1:14

Then God said, "Let lights appear in the sky to separate the day from the night. Let them mark off the seasons, days, and years.

Genesis 1 is an example of how using the lunar and solar phases,to account for the next Sabbat.

Nature itself becomes a source of wisdom,such as an invisible clock accounting for time.

We observe the lunar phases,A moon at its fullest is a time of great power and light.A time when things asked in prayer will surely be given..it is the start of something new in the cycle of life.

Psalm 104:19

You made the moon to mark the seasons,and the sun knows when to set.

Samhain: marks the new year,it is a time of remembering those who have gone on,our ancestors and also a time of acknowledging death to things that hold us back spiritual.It is not a time be be in fear,nor is it an evil time.

According to the Celts it observes the time that the veil between this word and the spirit world wanes the thinnest.

On this night October 31st the night shadows the day,night proceeds rather than follows the day.It is a time when the night comes much earlier getting ready for the shorter days between now and the Winter Solstice.

In this time of remeberance it is a solomn time,a time of recognition, reflection and reverence.The old is passed away and the new begins.

There is actually scripture showing that the Creator wants us to observe the Sabbats:

2 Chronicles 2:4

I am about to build a Temple to honor the name of the Lord my God. It will be a place set apart to burn fragrant incense before him, to display the special sacrificial bread, and to sacrifice burnt offerings each morning and evening, on the Sabbaths, at new moon celebrations, and at the other appointed festivals of the Lord our God.

He has commanded Israel to do these things forever.

Leviticus 26:10

You will have such a surplus of crops that you will need to clear out the old grain to make room for the new harvest!

This is also a metaphor for your spiritual life.

Yule:, being the second sabat is the Winter Solstice. This marks the longest night of the year. This Solstice is symbolic of the death and rebirth of the sun. As a Christopagan this Sabbat is also significant to the birth of Jesus.(Christmas)

In mythology,the Great mother gives birth to the Lord of Life..the

male aspect of Diety.

The land though barren with winter's blanket of snow..gives way to the evergreens that remind us that death is not forever,there is life beyond that everlasting and thriving.

As the Fir,Birch and Pines withstand the cold revealing the secret that there is a quality of thriving to life,even through the trials.

In the rest and reflection of winter.The Spirit symbolically hibernates getting ready for blooming in the spring.

A time to reflect on life and the sense of life giving way beneath the winter's cover of barrenness.Yule is a great example of life and death then resurrection that is promised to happen in time.

I must also mention the observance by some,of the Holly King and The Oak King.One old one new conquers the other to reign.The Oak King kills the Holly King and reigns until Midsummer,or Litha.Once the Summer Solstice arrives the two return to battle once more and reverse leadership.

The two symbolize the light and the dark twins. Not good and evil, but I am referring to darkness and light.

The Oak King represents, growth and expansion. The Holly king represents withdrawal, lessons, life and rest.

The Holly Bears the Crown

Holly stimulates the loving capacities of the heart by developing what Dr. Bach called "that great inner Self." Perhaps the most profound archetypal picture of Holly is evoked through its symbolism as the Crown of Thorns.

As the traditional Christmas carol proclaims, Of all the trees that are in the wood, the holly bears the crown.

"Druid priests wore Holly in their hair while collecting the sacred mistletoe medicine in the winter, Holly was also worn as a crown to represent the Holly King in seasonal festivals.

The Holly Crown was a sign of deepest respect and recognition that such an initiate had mastered the forces of nature in harmony with the human soul."(Christmas the Awakening Of The Heart, Edward Bach)

Imbolc :signals the middle of the season of long nights and anticipates the upcoming season of light.Spring in on the horizon new buds of life are sprouting from the once barren trees of winter.

There is a stirring of sorts of new life,rebirth and growth.The wishes and prayers sent out in the winter solstice are now giving way to new blessings and manifestations within the spiritual realm.

Also known as Candlemas associated with the goddess Brigid, who was later Christianised as St. Brigid.

Spring Equinox:celebrated around March 21st The word "equinox" derives from the Latin words meaning "equal night" and refers to the time when the sun crosses the equator. At such times, day and night are everywhere of nearly equal length everywhere in the world.Now is the time of balance between the growing light and the declining dark.

Significantly this Balance is also a time of balance within our own spirit. There has to be a balance of all things to create peace.

The earth gives way to a new harvest as we ourselves follow suit. The season is still that of an impending growth cycle of new life and abundance, spring; a time of birth. Also represents Easter, resurrection a sign of conquering death and beginning anew.

<u>Beltane</u>: This marks the beginning of summer. The land has given way to

fertility. All things are being born new at this time. The Breezes carry on them a sweet smell of nectar a time of joy, love and sexuality.

A time to honer fertility not only that of humans, animals, harvest.. but of the intellect, spirit, and heart. This is a time of the earth and it's inhabitants to become pregnant not only to create new life but, with a hope for tomorrow's blessings in their lives.

This time is when the veil is the thinnest between the physical and spiritual realm just as during the time of Samhain.

Beauty of life is celebrated, there is much joy about the fertility of hopes, dreams and aspirations.

Litha

Summer Solstice:This is the year's longest day.Celebrates youth and energy.Also known as Midsummer..we focus on the completeness of our achievements.Celebrating the life giving rays and warmth of the sun.

This is also the time the Oak King of summer(Life),is conquered by the Holly king of winter(Death)The two are actually dual to each other as a reflection of one.Without one the other cannot be.

Lughnasadh

Lughnasadh:also known as Lammas.This is the pre-cursor celebration of the harvest.Not only of the land but within ourselves.

Marking the beginning of fall harvest.The grain is cut, part of it goes into bread and nutrition, another part is stored away and used as seeds next spring, to create new life. Looking at that, thoughts about sacrifice, transformation, death and rebirth are also part of Lughnasadh.

"Feast of the First Fruits" anglosaxon 921 CE
The plant of Lughnasadh is any form of grain or corn.

Lughnasadh marks the begin of the noticeable descent of the Sun into the darkness of winter.

From the connection between the Earth (female principle) and the Sun (male principle), the marriage of the Sky Father (Sun God) with the Earth Mother we celebrated at Beltane, emerge the fruits of the first harvest of the year. Lughnasadh is a time of joy about the first fruits.

It is also a time of tension, because the dark days of winter are coming nearer, and most of the harvest is not brought in and stored away yet.

The God of the harvest is the Green Man (also known as John Barleycorn). He sacrifices himself every year in order to enable human life on Earth. In some areas his death is mourned with wreaths decorated with poppies or cornflowers.

"Jesus said, 'I am the bread of life; he who comes to me shall not hunger." (John 6:35)

"Wisdom speaks:'I am like a vine putting out graceful shoots,

 Approach me, you who desire me, And take your fill of my fruits…" (Ecclesiasticus 24: 17-19)

Exodus 23:16

"Celebrate the Festival of Harvest with the firstfruits of the crops you sow in your field. "Celebrate the Festival of Ingathering at the end of the year, when you gather in your crops from the field."

<u>Mabon</u>:" (MAY-bone or MAH-bawn) is named for the Welsh God and it is seen as the second of the three harvests, and particularly as a celebration o the vine harvests and of wine.

It is also associated with apples as symbols of life renewed.

Celebrating new-made wine, harvesting apples and vine products, and visiting burial cairns to place an apple upon them, were all ways in which the Celts honored this Sabbat. (Avalon, one of the many Celtic names for the Land of the Dead, literally means the "land of apples".)

These acts symbolized both thankfulness for the life-giving harvest, and the wish of the living to be reunited with their dead."

Taken from "Celtic Myth and Magick" by Edain McCoy

Also known as the Autumn Equinox, This is the moment when day (light) is equal to night (dark)

and balance is created between them. At the equinox, the sun rises directly in the east and sets directly in the west.

In the northern hemisphere, before the autumnal equinox, the sun rises and sets more and more to the north, and afterwards, it rises and sets more and more to the south.

Also called Harvest Home, this holiday is a ritual of thanksgiving for the fruits of the Earth and a recognition of the need to share them to secure the blessings of the Goddess and God during the winter months.

Among the sabbats, it is the second of the three harvest festivals, preceded by Lammas and followed by Samhain.

Mabon was not an authentic ancient festival either in name or date. The autumn equinox was not celebrated in Celtic countries, while all that is known about Anglo-Saxon customs of that time was that September was known as haleg-monath or 'holy month'

The Druids call this celebration, Mea'n Fo'mhair, and honor the The Green Man, the God of the Forest, by offering libations to trees.

Offerings of ciders, wines, herbs and fertilizer are appropriate at this time. Wiccans celebrate the aging Goddess as she passes from Mother to Crone, and her consort the God as he prepares for death and re-birth.

Tree Of Life

The concept of the Tree of Life is a wide spread subject. Many religions have used this to explain the idea that all life on earth in connected.

We all start out at the roots of the tree though different roots form it is the same tree.

According to the Encyclopedia Britannica, the tree of knowledge, connecting to heaven and the underworld, and the tree of life, connecting all forms of creation, are both forms of the world tree or cosmic tree.[1] According to some scholars, the tree of life and the tree of the knowledge of good and evil, portrayed in various religions and philosophies, are the same tree.

In the book of Proverbs the tree of life is associated with wisdom: "[Wisdom] is a tree of life to them that lay hold upon her, and happy is every one that holdest her fast." (Proverbs 3:13-18) In 15:4 the tree of life is associated with calmness: "A soothing tongue is a tree of life; but perverseness therein is a wound to the spirit."[5]

Yggdrasil

"In Norse mythology, Yggdrasil ("The Terrible One's Horse"), also called the World Tree, is the giant ash tree that links and shelters all the worlds.

Beneath the three roots the realms of Asgard, Jotunheim, and Niflheim are located. Three wells lie at its base: the Well of Wisdom (Mímisbrunnr), guarded by Mimir; the Well of Fate (Urdarbrunnr), guarded by the Norns; and the Hvergelmir (Roaring Kettle), the source of many rivers.

Four deer run across the branches of the tree and eat the buds; they represent the four winds.

There are other inhabitants of the tree, such as the squirrel Ratatosk ("swift teeth"), a notorious gossip, and Vidofnir ("tree snake"), the golden cock that perches on the topmost bough.

The roots are gnawed upon by Nidhogg and other serpents. On the day of Ragnarok, the fire giant Surt will set the tree on fire.

Other names for the tree include: Ask Yggdrasil, Hoddmimir's Wood, Laerad and Odin's Horse.

Old Norse: Mimameidr""Yggdrasil." Encyclopedia Mythica from Encyclopedia Mythica Online.

by Micha F. Lindemans

Article "Yggdrasil" created on 03 March 1997)

        Interestingly enough if we look at the metaphor of a tree,it cannot survive without a deep root system.The roots would become a symbol of the world.

There are many beliefs on how one should know God.

All these produce the trunk and the branches reach up to the heavens.

Speaking of those who would persecute another for their beliefs,or even kill in some cases. This represents an axe that tries to destroy the tree and chop it down. If the root system is strong enough the tree withstands all elements.

I believe as a society that is the way we should be, create a strong trunk without divisions, nurture what is within our hearts, not destroy. That spark of belief that lies within every individual, no man or woman can take away.

We are all striving to become enlightened to the ways of spirit. To grow and manifest in our own spiritual truths. Everyone's path is individually their own.

In the Gnostic Gospel of St. Thomas it clearly states "Let him who seeks continue seeking until he finds, When he finds, he will become troubled.

When he becomes troubled, he will be astonished, and he will rule over the all."

When we find our path to enlightenment, we are willing to be transformed in Spirit and in truth.

To open ones eyes to that which lies beyond dogmas, beyond the word of someone as human as we are behind a pulpit. That is when we decide to seek for ourself what and who wisdom is to us personally.

Those who criticize and judge others, even say "That is not how we believe, so it must be of the devil!"are simply blind to the concept that Spirit is within,it is not discovered by becoming content with what we have been told.

Glory is where you find it,the bible speaks to every individual differently.

I believe depending on what mountain you are ready to climb at the time of discovery.When I speak of this I am referring to the different lessons learned at the right time for the individual.

At times we must walk through the valleys before we are ready to pursue the mystery that is beyond the mountain!

Fear is not knowing or understanding ,to describe one's belief system in a negative sense is simply Fear.Bred out of ignorance and leads to strife.

Many wars have bee started because of divisions such as this,people have shed their blood for their beliefs.It is about time we all realize we come from the same tree!

Psalm 1:3

New King James Version (NKJV)

He shall be like a tree

>Planted by the rivers of water,

>That brings forth its fruit in its season,

Whose leaf also shall not wither;

And whatever he does shall prosper.

Jeremiah 17:8

For he shall be like a tree planted by the waters, Which spreads out its roots by the river,

And will not fear when heat comes; But its leaf will be green,

And will not be anxious in the year of drought, Nor will cease from yielding fruit.

Spiritual Meaning Of Various Trees

Apple:magick,youth,beauty

Ash:sacrifice,higher awareness,connection

Asphen:determination,courage,victory,transformation

Beech:hidden knowledge

Birch:new beginnings

Cedar:healing,cleansing, protection

Hawthorn:love,protection

Hazel:hidden wisdom

Holly:death,rebirth

Maple:balance,promise and prosperity

Oak is the mightiest of trees and symbolizes strength and courage.

The ancient Romans thought oak trees attracted lightening and thereby connected the oak tree to the sky god, Jupiter and his wife, Juno, the goddess of marriage. Thus, the oak is a symbol of conjugal fidelity and fulfillment.

The oak tree was regarded by Socrates as an oracle tree. The Druids likewise ate acorns in preparation for prophesying. In addition, the Druids believed the leaves of the oak tree had the power to heal and renew strength.

Palm:peace

Pine:creativity,immortality Some say the pine tree,gives off positivity to the spiritual enviornment.

Rowan:protection

Willow:magick,healing,intuition,dreams

Proverbs 13:13 - 18 states: Happy is the man that findeth wisdom, and the man that getteth understanding. For the merchandise of it is better than the merchandise of silver, and the gain thereof than fine gold.

 She is more precious than rubies: and all the things thou canst desire are not to be compared unto her.

Length of days is in her right hand; and in her left hand riches and honor. Her ways are ways of pleasantness, and all her paths are peace.

She is a tree of life to them that lay hold upon her: and happy is every one that retaineth her.

Coming To Know The Goddess

Growing up,I attended church with my grandmother.Every Sunday it was a common practice.

She would drive from thirty minutes away to bring me to the Church of Christ.

The extent of what I remember was not the preaching,the singing.It was simply her light.She magnified a room when she walked into it.

Her smile was authentic,which in this day is very rare to find.Her spirit was one of non-judgment,love for others and finding the good in everything and everyone.

This as I came to understand as I grew older was the making of someone true in spirit.

Authentic love and compassion through a child's eyes is easy to spot.Children still look beyond the veil of stigma,into the heart of others.

Into this reality people change as chameleons would through a child's perspective,unseen to most adults.They see the one thing the Creator wanted us all to see,the heart.

Luke 18:17

"Truly I tell you, anyone who will not receive the kingdom of God like a little child will never enter it."

As pagans,we study these various stories to gain insight into the spiritual world.

The concepts of Deity come from all these rolled into one message.This is the universal message that everything is connected,we are all part of the Divine,both male and female creating unity out of diversion.

Peace out of chaos.To consider the different personalities of the Greek,Egyptian,and others within mythology,we begin to understand the different personalities of Diety,learning life lessons we can take with us.

The various aspects of the God and Goddess show us how to be bold at times and humble at times.

Though God/Goddess has many faces in essence they all become the One.One of my good friends and mentors gave this analogy:"Seeing and understanding God is like the faucets of a diamond.

When the sun hits it,prisms of light are magnified in every direction with various colors and shapes.It is only one diamond reflecting infinite possibilities that are endless."Merddynn.

My grandmother also taught me life lessons threw the wisdom of nature.

Reflecting back,I can remember stories of marching ants,how they need the entire colony to survive and make a life for themselves.There are some that work,some that watch the young in all this is for the queen who holds the entire structure of the society in balance.

Ants though one of the smallest of creatures should be respected like everything in creation,for we can learn from all living things,the winds,plants and seasons.

These truths still resonate in my spirit,whether I realized it or not,she was my first teacher.

All things turn in unison,they are the essense of what makes up life as we know it.The birds sing their songs in the morning,to greet the sun.The night brings the shining moon and the owl's watchful eyes of wisdom give a sense of awareness that the wheel is still turning,night will not last forever and the morning will soon come.

The winds teach a lesson of invisibility,the wind is there although unseen to the eyes it is felt closing your eyes you can see it.

We all should realize how like the wind the Creator has no face,no gender.Who has ever seen God?We come from the days of the pictures in Sunday school,we get a visual that carries with us as we become older.

The Goddess is also alive,taken out of the sermons behind the pulpits over time,even wiped out of our bible,as early scholars and religious leaders decided for themselves what to keep and what to destroy.

We as women have been told not to speak up not to realize that we too are part of creation.Without female there can be no male.Things are born from the dual side.In this balance of duality we become a whole.

Her face is in the setting sun,the flowers of the field remind us of her beauty.The beauty that we too must embrace.The waters of life flow and ebb as they will and she as co-creator wills it done.

She is wisdom,the womb and the element of nurturing we all as humans yearn for.

Revelation 12:1 (KJV)

"And there appeared a great wonder in heaven; a woman clothed with the sun, and the moon under her feet, and upon her head a crown of twelve stars"

In Hebrew the word "Spirit" is feminine. This is a very interesting concept.

In the scent of the rose, I am there.

Thoughts on the Goddess:

Though time turns the page, my fire still burns

I am the wind, in your hair

The sun warm -upon your skin.

The whispers within your spirit,in the light of the moon

I shadow you with my wings

with a love in bloom

I am the first bird, of morning as it sings.

My voice is within

down deep in the forest,under an old oak tree

calling of things that once have been.

Open the eyes of your heart to see.

I am she,Wisdom of old..seek me,know me,feel me,rest in my arms ,as you dream..

know in the morning,you shall hear my song again

feel the warmth of my kiss,smell the scent of my love,taste the sweetness of my fruit,look into your reflection,

I am there looking back..between veils of time and space,through the shadows I am the light.I am Love..

the only mystery you seek is within,so know dear child..you have the key..you are free.

According the Carl Jung there are two types of archetypes to the human beings,maleness and femalness,which he believe existed in both sexes.

The *anima* represented the female archetype in men;the *animus* represented the masculine archetype in woman.There has to be a balance of the two to create a whole person.

To seek after the Goddess figure as a woman was to me,an empowerment.I grew to understand who I was as a woman,made in the image of the Spirit of the Creator,which had me also in mind as a Creation.

As I have discussed in previous chapters,There can be a mother and a father.It is a law of nature and to me also a concept in my beliefs.

I rationalize these in my psyche.In my prayerful mind,I can see the two standing as royalty watching over me.

I believe it was here,I first came to understand life principles in

their true nature.The world was not about who was wrong or right,

it was a deeper meaning one that you could only come to understand through

the eyes and heart of a child.Children hold
    the key to the purity

of life.They have not yet been conditioned
    to judge,but grasp the truth

for what it is,a simplicity that comes from
    understanding the world

around them,how it ticks,why is the sky
    blue,what is the emotion or

feeling you get from that blue.If someone
    tells you to eat your vegetables,

a child will hesitate from the unknown.As
    the parent urges them on gently

they come to see that a brocoli is not so
    terrible after all with a

little cheese.This is an analogy of how we
    all seem to be today.

People tell you something is evil just
    because they themselves have

never took the time to seek it for
    themselves.

The Christian church conferred the Goddess's title as the Mother of Jesus. They called Her,"Mary, Queen of Heaven" and "Mary, Queen of the Angels"

The Nag Hammadi Library, a collection of thirteen ancient codices containing over fifty texts, was discovered in upper Egypt in 1945.

This immensely important discovery includes a large number of primary "Gnostic Gospels" -- texts once thought to have been entirely destroyed during the early Christian struggle to define "orthodoxy" -- scriptures such as the Gospel of Thomas, the Gospel of Philip, and the Gospel of Truth.

Early Christianity & the Gospel of Mary

Few people today are acquainted with the Gospel of Mary. Written early in the second century CE, it disappeared for over fifteen hundred years until a single, fragmentary copy in Coptic translation came to light in the late nineteenth century.

Although details of the discovery itself are obscure, we do know that the fifth-century manuscript in which it was inscribed was purchased in Cairo by Carl Reinhardt and brought to Berlin in 1896.

Two additional fragments in Greek have come to light in the twentieth century. Yet still no complete copy of the Gospel of Mary is known. Fewer than eight pages of the ancient papyrus text survive, which means that about half of the Gospel of Mary is lost to us, perhaps forever.

Yet these scant pages provide an intriguing glimpse into a kind of Christianity lost for almost fifteen hundred years.

This astonishingly brief narrative presents a radical interpretation of Jesus' teachings as a path to inner spiritual knowledge; it rejects his suffering and death as the path to eternal life; it exposes the erroneous view that Mary of Magdala was a prostitute for what it is-a piece of theological fiction; it presents the most straightforward and convincing argument in any early Christian writing for the legitimacy of women's leadership; it offers a sharp critique of illegitimate power and a utopian vision of spiritual perfection; it challenges our rather romantic views about the harmony and unanimity of the first Christians; and it asks us to rethink the basis for church authority. All written in the name of a woman.

The story of the Gospel of Mary is a simple one. Since the first six pages are lost, the gospel opens in the middle of a scene portraying a discussion between the Savior and his disciples set after the resurrection.

The Savior is answering their questions about the end of the material world and the nature of sin. He teaches them that at present all things, whether material or spiritual, are interwoven with each other. In the end, that will not be so.

Each nature will return to its own root, its own original state and destiny. But meanwhile, the nature of sin is tied to the nature of life this mixed world.

People sin because they do not recognize their own spiritual nature and, instead, love the lower nature that deceives them and leads to disease and death.

Salvation is achieved by discovering within oneself the true spiritual nature of humanity and overcoming the deceptive entrapments of the bodily passions and the world.

The Savior concludes this teaching with a warning against those who would delude the disciples into following some heroic leader or a set of rules and laws. Instead they are to seek the child of true Humanity within themselves and gain inward peace. After commissioning them to go forth and preach the gospel, the Savior departs.

But the disciples do not go out joyfully to preach the gospel; instead controversy erupts. All the disciples except Mary have failed to comprehend the Savior's teaching Rather than seek peace within, they are distraught, frightened that if they follow his commission to preach the gospel, they might share his agonizing fate.

Mary steps in and comforts them and, at Peter's, relates teaching unknown to them that she had received from the Savior in a vision.

The Savior had explained to her the nature of prophecy and the rise of the soul to its final rest, describing how to win the battle against the wicked, illegitimate Powers that seek to keep the soul entrapped in the world and ignorant of its true spiritual nature.

But as she finishes her account, two of the disciples quite unexpectedly challenge her. Andrew objects that her teaching is strange and he refuses to believe that it came from the Savior.

Peter goes for her, denying that Jesus would ever have given this kind of advanced teaching to a woman, or that Jesus could possibly have preferred her to them.

Apparently when he asked her to speak, Peter had not expected such elevated teaching, and now he questions her character, implying that she has lied about having received special teaching in order to increase her stature among the disciples. Severely taken aback, Mary begins to cry at Peter's accusation.

Levi comes quickly to her defense, pointing out to Peter that he is a notorious hothead and now he is treating Mary as though she were the enemy.

We should be ashamed of ourselves, he admonishes them all; instead of arguing among ourselves, we should go out and preach the gospel as the Savior commanded us.

The story ends here, but the controversy is far from resolved. Andrew and Peter at least, and likely the other fearful disciples as well, have not understood the Savior's teaching and are offended by Jesus' apparent preference of a woman over them.

Their limited understanding and false pride make it impossible for them to comprehend the truth of the Savior's teaching. The reader must both wonder and worry what kind of gospel such proud and ignorant disciples will preach.

How are we to understand this story? It is at once reminiscent of the New Testament gospels and yet clearly different from them. The gospel's characters-the Savior, Mary, Peter, Andrew, and Levi-are familiar to those acquainted with the gospels of Matthew, Mark, Luke, and John.

So, too, is the theological language of gospel and kingdom, as well as such sayings of

Jesus as "Those who seek will find" or "Anyone with two ears should listen."

New Testament gospels and Acts repeatedly mention the appearance of Jesus to his disciples after the resurrection.

Yet it is also clear that the story of the Gospel of Mary differs in significant respects.

For example, after Jesus commissions the disciples they do not go out joyfully to preach the gospel, as they do in Matthew; instead they weep, fearing for their lives. Some of the teachings also seem shocking coming from Jesus, especially his assertion that there is no such thing as sin. Modern read-ers may well find themselves sympathizing with Andrew's assessment that "these teachings are strange ideas."

The Gospel of Mary was written when Christianity, still in its nascent stages, was made up of communities widely dispersed around the Eastern Mediteranean, communities which were often relatively iso-la ted from one other and probably each small enough to meet in someone's home without attracting too much notice.

Although writings appeared early-especially letters addressing the concerns of local churches, collections containing Jesus' sayings, and narratives interpreting his death and resurrection—oral practices dominated the lives of early Christians. Preaching, teaching, and rituals of table fellowship and baptism were the core of the Christian experience?

What written documents they had served at most as supplemental guides to preaching and practice. Nor can we assume that the various churches all possessed the same documents; after all, these are the people who wrote the first Christian literature. Christoph Markschies suggests that we have lost 85% of Christian literature from the first two centuries–and that includes only the literature we know about.

Surely there must be even more, for the discovery of texts like the Gospel of Mary came as a complete surprise.

We have to be careful that we don't suppose it is possible to reconstruct the whole of early Christian history and practice out of the few surviving texts that remain.

Our picture will always be partial—not only because so much is lost, but because early Christian practices were so little tied to durable writing.

Partly as a consequence of their independent development and differing situations, these churches sometimes diverged widely in their perspectives on essential elements of Christian belief and practice.

Such basic issues as the content and meaning of Jesus' teachings, the nature of salvation, the value of prophetic authority, and the roles of women and slaves came under intense debate.

Early Christians proposed and experimented with competing visions of ideal community.

It is important to remember, too, that these first Christians had no New Testament, no Nicene Creed or Apostles Creed, no commonly established church order or chain of authority, no church buildings, and indeed no single understanding of Jesus.

All of the elements we might consider to be essential to define Christianity did not yet exist. Far from being starting points, the Nicene creed and the New Testament were the end products of these debates and disputes; they represent the distillation of experience and experimentation—and not a small amount of strife and struggle.

All early Christian literature bears traces of these controversies. The earliest surviving documents of Christianity, the letters of Paul show that considerable difference of opinion existed about such issues as circumcision and the Jewish food laws or the relative value of spiritual gifts.

These and other such contentious issues as whether the resurrection was physical or spiritual were stimulating theological conversations and causing rifts within and among Christian groups.

By the time of the Gospel of Mary, these discussions were becoming increasingly nuanced and more polarized.

History, as we know, is written by the winners. In the case of early Christianity, this has meant that many voices in these debates were silenced through repression or neglect. The Gospel of Mary, along with other newly discovered works from the earliest Christian period, increases our knowledge of the enormous diversity and dynamic character of the processes by which Christianity was shaped.

The goal of this volume is to let twenty-first-century readers hear one of those voices—not in order to drown out the voices of canon and tradition, but in order that they might be heard with the greater clarity that comes with a broadened historical perspective.

Whether or not the message of the Gospel of Mary should be embraced is a matter readers will decide for themselves.

Discovery and Publication

Where did the Gospel of Mary come from?

Over a hundred years ago, in January of 1896, a seemingly insignificant event took place on the antiquities market in Cairo. A manuscript dealer, whose name history has forgotten, offered a papyrus book for sale to a German scholar named Dr. Carl Reinhardt.?

It eventually became clear that the book was a fifth-century CE papyrus codex, written in the Coptic language.

Unbeknownst to either of them, it contained the Gospel of Mary along with three other previously unknown works, the Apocryphon of John, the Sophia of Jesus Christ, and the Act of Peter. This seemingly small event turned out to be of enormous significance.

Dr. Reinhardt could tell that the book was ancient, but he knew nothing more about the find than that the dealer was from Achmim in central. The dealer told him that a peasant had found the book in a niche of a wall, but that is impossible.

The book's excellent condition, except for several pages missing from the Gospel of Mary, makes it entirely unlikely that it had spent the last fifteen hundred years unnoticed in a wall niche.

No book could have survived so long in the open air. It may be that the peasant or the dealer had come by it illegally and, hence, was evasive about the actual location of the find. Or it may have been only recently placed in the wall and accidentally found there. In any case, we still don't know anything specific about where it lay hidden all those centuries, although the first editor, Carl Schmidt, assumed that it had to have been found in the graveyards of Achmim or in the area surrounding the city.

Dr. Reinhardt purchased the book and took it to Berlin, where it was placed in the Egyptian Museum with the official title and catalogue number of Codex Berolinensis 8502. There it came into the hands of the Egyptologist Can Schmidt, who set about producing a critical edition and German translation of what is now generally referred to as the Berlin Codex

From the beginning, the publication was plagued by difficulties. First of all, there is the problem of the missing pages. The first six pages, plus four additional pages from the middle of the work, are missing. This means that over half of the Gospel of Mary is completely lost.

What happened to these pages? Carl Schmidt thought they must have been stolen or destroyed by whoever found the book. The man itself was found protected inside its original leather and papyrus cover but by the time it reached Carl Schmidt in Berlin, the order of the pages had been The considerably jumbled. It took Schmidt some time to realize that the book was nearly intact and must therefore have been found uninjured.

In an uncharitable and perhaps even rancorous comment, Schmidt attributed the disorder of the pages to "greedy Arabs" who must also have either stolen or destroyed the missing pages, but to this day nothing is known about their fate. We can only hope that they

lie protected somewhere and will one day resurface.

By 1912 Schmidt's edition was ready for publication and was sent to the Prießchen Press in Leipzig. But alas! The printer was nearing completion of the final sheets when a burst water pipe destroyed the entire edition.

Soon thereafter Europe plunged into World War I. During the war and its aftermath, Schmidt was unable to go to Leipzig and salvage anything from the mess himself, but he did manage to resurrect the project.

This time, however, his work was thwarted by his own mortality. His death on April 17, 1938, caused further delay while the edition was retrieved from his estate and sent to press. At this point, another scholar was needed to see its publication through, a task that ultimately fell to Walter Till in 1941.

In the meantime, in 1917 a small third-century Greek fragment of the Gospel of Mary had been found in Egypt (Papyrus Rylands 463). Being parallel to

part of the Coptic text, it added no new passages to the Gospel of Mary, but it did provide a few variants and additional evidence about the work's early date and its composition in Greek. Till incorporated this new evidence into his edition, and by 1943, the edition was again ready to go to press. But now World War II made publication impossible.

By the time the war was over, news had reached Berlin of a major manuscript discovery in Egypt near the village of Nag Hammadi.

As chance would have it, copies of two of the other texts found within the Berlin Codex along with the Gospel of Mary (Apocryphon of John and Sophia of Jesus Christ) appeared among the new manuscripts.

No new copies of Gospel of Mary were found at Nag Hammadi, but publication was delayed yet again as Till waited for information about the new manuscripts so that he could incorporate this new evidence into his edition of the Berlin Codex. But the wheels of scholarship grind slowly, and finally in exasperation, Till gave up. He confides to his readers:

In the course of the twelve years during which I have labored over the texts, I often made repeated changes here and there, and that will probably continue to be the case. But at some point a man must find the courage to let the manuscript leave one's hand, even if one is convinced that there is much that is still imperfect.

That is unavoidable with all human endeavors.

At last in 1955, the first printed edition of the text of the Gospel of Mary finally appeared with a German translation.

Till was right, of course; scholars continue to make changes and add to the record. Of foremost importance was the discovery of yet another early third-century Greek fragment of the Gospel of Mary(Papyrus Oxyrhynchus 3525),

which was published in 1983. With the addition of this fragment, we now have portions of three copies of the Gospel of Mary dating from antiquity: two Greek manuscripts from the early third century (P. Rylands 463 and P. Oxyrhynchus 3525) and one in Coptic from the fifth century (Codex Berolinensis 8525).

Because it is unusual for several copies from such early dates to have survived, the attestation of the Gospel of Mary as an early Christian work is unusually strong.

Most early Christian literature that we know about has survived because the texts were copied and then recopied as the materials on which they were written wore out.

In antiquity it was not necessary to burn books one wanted to suppress (although this was occasionally done); if they weren't recopied, they disappeared through neglect. As far as we know, the Gospel of Mary was never recopied after the fifth century; it may have been that the Gospel of Mary was actively suppressed, but it is also possible that it simply dropped out of circulation.

Either way, whether its loss resulted from animosity or neglect, the recovery of the Gospel of Mary, in however fragmentary condition, is due in equal measure to phenomenal serendipity and extraordinary good fortune.

Dr. King's outline of the surviving manuscript fragments:

The Coptic Language

Although the Gospel of Mary was originally composed in Greek, most of

it survives only in Coptic translation. Coptic is the last stage of the Egyptian language and is still in liturgical use by Egyptian Christians, called Copts.

The oldest known Egyptian language was written in hieroglyphs, always on stone or some other durable material. In addition, Egyptians

also wrote on papyrus, and for this they used a different script called hieratic, employed almost solely for writing sacred literature. A third script, called demotic, was developed for everyday transactions like letter-writing and book-keeping. Each of these scripts is very cumbersome, utilizing different characters or signs to represent whole syllables, not just individual sounds as in English.

Sometime during the late Roman period, probably around the second century CE, scribes started writing the Egyptian language in primarily Greek letters, but adding a few from demotic Egyptian.

This process made writing Egyptian much simpler and more efficient. Since Coptic script was used almost exclusively by Christians in Egypt, we can assume that Egyptian Christians were the ones who translated and preserved the Gospel of Mary.

The Berlin Codex

The book Reinhardt bought in Cairo in 1896 turned out to be a fifth-century papyrus codex.

Papyrus was the most common writing material of the day, but codices, the precursor of our book form, had come into use only a couple of centuries earlier, primarily among Christians.

The codex was made by cutting papyrus rolls into sheets, which then were stacked in a single pile, usually made up of at least 38 sheets. Folding the pile in half and sewing the sheets together produced a book of about 152 pages, which was finally placed inside a leather cover.

The Gospel of Mary is a short work, taking up only the first 18⅔ pages of a codex that itself is relatively small in size, having leaves that measure on average only about 12.7 cm long and 10.5 cm wide.

Papyrus Rylands 463 (PRyl)

This Greek fragment of the Gospel of Mary was acquired by the Rylands Library in Manchester, England, in 1917, and published in 1938 by C. H. Roberts.

Like POxy 3525, it was found at Oxyrhynchus in northern Egypt, and dates to the early third century CE. It is a fragment from a codex—it has writing on both sides of the papyrus leaf—and exhibits a very clear literary script.

It measures 8.7 cm wide by 10 cm long, although most fibers measure only 8.5. cm.

The front of the fragment contains the conclusion of Mary's revelation and the beginning of the disciples' dispute over her teaching. After a short gap, the dispute continues on the other side of the fragment and ends with Levi leaving to announce the good news (GMary 9:29-10:4; 10:6-14).

Papyrus Oxyrhynchus 3525 (POxy)

This tiny and severely damaged papyrus fragment of the Gospel of Mary in Greek was found during excavations of the town of Oxyrhynchus, along the Nile in lower (northern) Egypt. Published in 1983 by P. J. Parsons, it is now housed in the Ashmolean Library at Oxford. I

t dates to the early third century CE. The fragment has writing on only one side, indicating that it came from a roll, not a codex (book).

Because it was written in a cursive Greek script usually reserved for such documentary papyri as business documents and letters rather than literary texts, Parsons suggested that it was the work of an amateur.

What remains is a very fragmentary fragment indeed. It contains approximately twenty lines of writing, none of them complete. The papyrus measures 11.7 cm long and is 11.4 cm at its widest point, but the top half is only about 4 cm wide.

The restoration is based largely on the parallel Coptic text. It contains the Savior's farewell, Mary's comforting of the other disciples, Peter's request to Mary to teach, and the beginning of her vision (GMary 4:11-7:3).

Excerpt from:

The Gospel of Mary of Magdala: Jesus and the First Woman Apostle

by Karen L. King (Polebridge Press, Santa Rosa, California, 2003)

Our prehistoric ancestors were hunters and gatherers, who depended on the earth to provide, food, clothing, shelter and life itself. The importance of fertility in crops, in domesticated animals, in wild animals and in the tribe itself were of paramount importance to their survival.

Their society was probably matriarchal and that children took their mothers' names. Their life was based on lunar (not solar) calendar and time was experienced as a repetitive cycle, not linearly as we think of it today.

Thus, the Female life-giving principle was considered divine and shrouded in mystery.

Natures Mother who bringest all to life and revives

all from day to day. The food of life Thou grantest in

eternal fidelity. And when the soul hath retired we

take refuge in Thee. All that Thou grantest falls

back somewhere into Thy Womb.

Third Century AD Prayer to Terra Matris.

Cave paintings and rock carvings of Goddesses, some as old as 35,000 years B.C.E. or earlier, depict the Divine life-giving Goddess.

The Venus of Willendorf, is perhaps the most well known of these ancient Mother-Goddess deities, most of the early images of the Goddess show an abundant, round, full figured being. An early symbol in human history is the zig-zag, which was used by Neanderthals around 40,000 B.C. and has been interpreted as representing water. The Goddess is closely associated with water and births.

In medieval times, it was claimed that Britain was given to their ancestors by the Goddess Diana. In 1136, Geoffrey of Monmouthshire, describes in his "History of The Kings Of Britain" how refugees escaping the siege of Troy, were seeking a new homeland. Their leader called upon Diana to help them:

" O powerful Goddess,

terror of the forest glades,

yet hope of the wild woodland,

you, who have the power to go into orbit,

though the airy heavens and halls of hell,

pronounce a judgment that concerns the Earth.

Tell me which lands you wish us to inhabit.

Tell me of a safe dwelling-place,

where I am to worship you down the ages,

and where, to the chanting of maidens,

I shall dedicate temples to you. "

In the ancient world, Goddesses were commonly patronesses of cities, justice, was, handicraft and home life, agriculture, love and learning.

They were seen as standing for aspects of human nature and civilization rather than that of nature and the elements.

Apuleius in his work Metamorphoses, declared that Isis was the embodiment of all other Goddesses and identified with the Moon and nature. It would be this concept of the Goddess that would become dominant in modern paganism.

The faces and aspects of the Goddess are not static or frozen in time but are forever changing, evolving and metamorphosing. In each age, like children growing, so the Goddess grows and changes with us.

So it was during the years 1300-1800, in English love poetry, the most popular Goddesses were Venus - Goddess of Love, Diana - Goddess of Chastity and Hunting, Minerva - Goddess of Wisdom, and Juno as a symbol of Queenliness.

After the 1800's Juno is replaced by Proserpine - Goddess of the Seasons or the Dead, by 1830 Minerva is replaced by Cere or Demeter - Lady of The Harvest.

The Goddess Venus also undergoes changes during this time, acquiring dominion over the woodland or the sea, and Diana becomes associated with the Moon, the greenwood and wild animals.

    Coming to understand the Goddess is
        already planted within us,at

  conception we depend on our mother to
        sustain us.At birth she nurtures

  us,taught us as we age.This nurture aspect is
        within male and female,it is

what makes us into great parents,loyal
        companions to one another,and gives

us the ability to see the world in a
        compassionate way.

As I see the Goddess,she is what is reflected within myself.Divine femininity.That seeks to

protect and nurture.She is the dual aspect of God,the balance between what creates and what destroys only to bring to life once more.

Several years ago,I was attending a Sunday service.This was a church I had never been to.

Through my journey I saught after what was and what wasn't through every denomination.I was open-minded to hear all forms of beliefs from each denomination.

The pastor was preaching and out of nowhere made the statement"And some people think God is a Woman!"I believe he was teaching on false prophets..the congregation gasped,in a manner that it was unheard of or an evil thing.It made me think of the Catholic church,was it such a shock for them to acknowledge Mary?Who by the way originated from the Goddess of the Old Ways.

Unknowingly,the pastor was wording this statement wrong,not that woman is the god by an aspect of the Diety.The Spirit of the Creator is both gender,if we stop to look at the wisdom that is within nature all things are born with both parents,not just a male.The Lord and the Lady make up what is "US"

As in scripture where it speaks of the two becoming one.Both come together to form completion.It is within the framework of the laws of nature,within ying/yang within all humans male and female DNA.

Through centuries society forgot the Goddess,attempted to erase her.What is this ancient and also Divine cannot be erased within the truths deep within our spirit.

Let's consider the Egyptians.The Egyptians explained how creation began from the nature they saw around them. The largest elements were the Nile River and the sun, so each of these played a major part in the creation story.

As with most cultures, the story of the creation of the world was passed down from generation to generation .A grandfather may have told his grandchildren something of this nature:A Version of the Egyptian Story

Come, children. It is time to learn where you came from and who you should honor to for it.

Long ago, before there was anything that you see now, there was Nu. He was the Great Waters. Deep within him lived eight gods known as Ogdoad.

They were Nun and Nunet who were gods of the deep waters. Heh and Hehet ruled the endless space. Kek and Keket controlled darkenss. Amon and Amonet ruled all that was invisible. They were guard the Great Egg in which the Creator slept.

Eventually the Great Egg started to crack. It split in two and divided the Nun into two parts: what you hear us call the Upper and the Lower. In between the parts, a space was left so that the Creator could begin to create the rest of the world.

A large blue Lotus rose up from the egg and passed through the deep

waters. Once it had risen above the waters, it opened its petals to reveal the Creator, Amen-Re. Light shone from Amen-Re and pushed darkness to the ends of the universe. He rose up into the space and released the loudest cry that ended the silence that had always been. From this sound, Toth, the god of wisdom was created.

Amon-Re then returned to the space that was left between the Upper and Lower and created an island to call home. As time went on he realized that being alone can be painful. So, he began to create everything else.

The Creator first created Maat, the goddess of Balance, Truth, and Justice. the wife of Thoth and together wisdom and truth ruled. The creator continue He realized how important this would be for all creation. Maat became d to create other beings and giving them authority.

There was the god of air, Shu. He created the goddess of moisture, Tefnut.

Amon-Re still felt very alone. So, he reached up and removed one of his eyes became the goddess of the sky and was given a place of honor in Amon-Re's forehead taking the shape of the great cobra that you know as the Uraeus serpent.and from it created his daughter. Hathor

Shu took Tefnut as a wife and twins were given to them, Geb the god of earth and Nut, goddess of the heavens. Amon-Re took Nut

for his wife though in her heart she wanted
her brother, Geb, to be her husband.

They began to meet secretly not knowing
the chaos they were causing. Amon-Re
discovered them on day and in anger
separated them. He pushed sky way above
the earth. Shu was placed between them to
prevent any more encounters.

But the chaos still remained. Re discovered
  that his wife was to have

children by Geb. He punished her by
  preventing her from ever giving birth.

The children would stay within her forever.
  Nut was devastated that she

could not be with her lover and could not
  hold her children in her arms.

Her loud cries penetrated the whole
  universe. Thoth, the god of wisdom,

heard her cries and began to search for a
  way to comfort her. He decided

to challenge the mood goddess, Silene, into
  risking a part of her light

for each day of the year. He won the wager
  which is why as the month goes

on you will see Silene's glow grow smaller
  and smaller. He took the light

he won and when all those little pieces of
light were put together, five extra days
were created that he could add to the year.
Since these days

were not part of the original creation of Re
and did not fall into any

of the months Re ordained, Thoth found a
way for Nut to give birth to her children. So
on each of those five days, Nut gave birth
to a child.

Day 1 was Osiris. Day 2 was Elder Horus.
Day 3 was Set who was the god

of warfare. Day 4 was Isis who was the
goddess of love. Day 5 was Nephthys.

Osiris took Isis as his wife; and Set took
        Nephthys as his wife.

Over time Re began to create other gods and
many spirits and demons. Eventually, Re
created Man and all the animals on the
earth. He created

the land of Khemet or Egypt and placed man
there. Re placed the desert

around man to protect him and the Nile was
to flood the earth to provide

rich soil.

Search within your divine feminity,seek out the mother,the maiden and crone.

These three are a metaphor for the different stages a woman goes threw before reaching maturity.

- Maiden, aspect is always first representing:Newness, youth, purity, and innocence.

- Mother, a woman who has reached puberty, represents the second stage. Her role is one of fertility, growth,childbearing.In this aspect she has left the maiden stage and becomes more settled,focused on nurture.

- The Crone, an elderly woman, represents the last phase. She is symbolic of wisdom, experience, change, transformation and death.

As with the Lord,the Lady aspects are seen to teach life lessons,experience the harvests of life.The blooming of life as well as it's wisdom.

Again,there are many names for goddesses in the past myths.We tend to see the all as one again..different personalities for a single.

They all have different attributes,some warriors,some relate to home and hearth,others of peace and newness.

Known as Wisdom,Isis,Mary,Diana,Heckate just to cover a few.

With the Lord aspect of Diety She defines a new wholeness.Just as two colors such as blue(god)and pink(goddess)create violet.The Trinity of both the God/Goddess come together to define ONE.

A good search would be in the book of Proverbs,:

- Proverbs 8:12

"I, Wisdom, live together with good judgment.I know where to discover knowledge and discernment."

- Proverbs 9:1

"Wisdom has built her house;she has carved its seven columns."

- Proverbs 3:18

"Wisdom is a tree of life to those who embrace her;happy are those who hold her tightly."

Five Principles Of Intimate Prayer

To Know:Belief in ourselves is sometimes stifled by the day to day struggle to balance a spiritual life,career life,and family life.

Finding time to slow down is difficult at times,but it is possible.

When we Know ourselves we are truly empowered.,Plato went into the deep meaning of this quote.Long-established wisdom.In life we learn lessons from our achievements as well as our mistakes.

We come to know our boundaries,what we are capable of.To have full self-assurance,without doubt.

Introspection:self-observation and reporting of conscious inner thoughts, desires and sensations. It is a conscious and purposive process relying on thinking, reasoning, and examining one's own thoughts, feelings, and, in more spiritual cases, one's soul.

It can also be called contemplation of one's self, and is contrasted with extrospection, the observation of things external to one's self. Introspection may be used synonymously with and in a similar way to human self-reflection. It is used greatly as a spiritual examination.

This is achieved through daily meditation.Any destination to knowing your true self takes time and effort,we are all in the process of becoming.To reach that full potential.

In psychology,the shadow self-is a part of us that is primal,the fear factor within human nature.This must be faced and compromised with.

When we face our fears and journey threw our shadow selves we learn incredible lessons in courage,we become warriors with a part of us that has long been hidden.

According to Carl Jung(1967),all humans share a vast collective unconscious,containing universal memories,symbols and images that pass through our DNA through history.

To break the chain-reaction of fear,guilt,shame it is important to take a look within our own psyche.

Overcome these spots that are in our spirit.Let go of all the labels that one has heard themselves being called all their life.You are not defined by a label!Only canned goods have this right,You are created perfect. It is true we have issues with our past as Jung said.

Truly Know that you are of self-worth and have the spirit of the Creator.

It is in our own thoughts, how we come to Know ourselves. In Proverbs 23, it clearly states "as a man thinketh so is he" A thought-form is a manifestation of mental energy, saying this what think manifests who we are. It also defines how we see the world we live in.

Someone who keeps a negative attitude, actually damages their health. Ulcers, high-blood pressure..ect. The body follows suit with the brain's thought manifestation.

Someone who is empathic can suffer side effects from relating to negative minded individuals.

Empaths know when they enter a room others who are open to speak to, they feel the sadness, pain, or joy from individuals.

This all derives from thought-forms. So much energy is manifested, the emotion is felt by others.

This is why at times you meet a person you feel you could speak to forever, you get a good feeling around that person. Other times you feel that closed up feeling.

These thought-forms reflected in the energy fields of others or auras are powerful.Thoughts become things,Keep them Positive!

Then you truly Know yourself,with introspective,meditation,and prayer.Know that you are a spiritual being with power,then believe it,really believe it!

In the world of Metaphysics..energy is defined as the invisible force that we ourselves create.With this we can move mountains.It's all about faith,faith in yourself.Scientific laws also relate to this.

Energy sent out brings forth that from the nature it came,positive or negative.

Awareness of self,in what you pray for know that once it goes out into the universe,the Creator goes into action.

To Will:To send out prayer is another form of magick within itself.I have heard it said "some know it as miracles and others call it as magick"These are the same principle.

Offering up your intent with the knowledge and wisdom that you have gathered your thoughts of focus and intent.To will something is simply to believe it has already came to pass.Directing your deep down passions,emotions,intent toward the final goal.

Imagine an arrow pointed toward your goal then point and shoot.

To Dare:To dare is putting your will into action.Dare to have faith within yourself to bring change to any situation.

Dare to know yourself well enough to believe with all your heart,mind,and emotions to harness them to create a reaction.It takes courage to dare to dream of the life you could have,instead of dreaming-know that it has already came into being.I

t is up to you as an individual to have the courage to know you are the only one who can shape your own reality,no one can achieve this for you here on earth but you.

You are the creator of your life,the quality of it.Know your abilities and dare to be who you were created to be.Dare to put for action to manifest change.

Keep Silent:Once you have put your goal into action,you believe it has come to pass.

Take up the scipture"Be still and KNOW I am God"Don't dwell on it,speak of it just go with the wisdom that it is as it is.The universe will answer in due time one way or another.

When you speak of a prayer sent out you dilute the magick of faith within yourself.

To speak of something or to question it is doubt.Go forth with no doubt.Send it out and seal it as done.

Imagine:To see the final conclusion of the prayer you sent out,wraps it all up.You have to visualize the outcome to create the final conclusion.If you can see it,it is already accomplished within your mind,heart,and spirit.

This makes the desire burn brighter in the psyche,creating it then in reality.Here is the key to the other four.It all starts within our own Imagination.

What we think becomes reality if we have faith in it.

According to metaphysics, in order to manifest something ,three components must come together.

These components are time,space,and energy.Accordingly,if someone selects a space,and a time,then directs energy there(prayer),a manifestation occurs.

The three stages of prayer are as follows:

- Oral-spoken word,we use our breath to speak thus releasing the essense of spirit into the metaphysical plane.

- Focused Intent-meditative prayer,can be chants.Some Christians chant the name maranatha to call upon Jesus.Our level of focus determines the outcome of our desires to become reality.

- Heart Prayer-Is not in what we do or say,it is how we say it from the innermost depths of our being.

Theosis is the search for an intimate union with the Divine within the depths of your being.It is being face to face with Diety.Just as the apostles were with Jesus.

An interesting concept,Jesus had twelve apostles including Himself equals the number of thirteen;this is the same number of a coven.

The word was originally a late medieval Scots word (circa 1500) meaning a gathering of any kind.

Symbols That Define Faith

The Pentagram

Is a five pointed star, encased in a circle. It represents the five Elements of the Wise. It is also the symbol of the perfected human being.

The four elements of material creation are surmounted by the fifth Element Of Spirit, the element that links us to the Divine.

The five Impressions of the Great Light are found represented within

the *Esoteric Pentagram*.

The *Gnostic Pentagram* is the human figure with four limbs, and one

unique apex which is the head.

The circle being a symbol of eternity and infinity, the cycles of life and nature.

The circle touching all 5 points indicates that the spirit, earth, air, water and fire are all connected.

Up until medieval times, the five points of the pentagram represented the five wounds of Christ on the Cross. It was a symbol of Christ the Saviour.

The pentagram has long been believed to be a potent protection against evil, a symbol of conflict that shields the wearer and the home. The pentagram has five spiked wards and a womb shaped defensive, protective pentagon at the center.

The Pentagram, which in Gnostic schools is known as the Flaming Star, is the sign of magic omnipotence.

The five Impressions of the Great Light and the five Helpers are contained within the Flaming Star. The five Helpers are the five Genii: Gabriel, Raphael, Uriel, Michael, and Samuel.

Unfortunately this symbol has had negative feedback with many Christians.Media and heresay has made this symbol a form of evil.

It is unsure where the false beliefs came from,there have been countless times I have been wearing my pentacle and a Christian friend or two of mine,would see it and gasp with a look of fear on their face.

Many never knew this was the original symbol of the Christian faith.Strange how one symbol can get so much of a reaction,after all stars are everywhere.

Any law officer wearing their badge has probably never had this issue.The form of an emblem to the law officer means to serve and protect.A circle signifies Eternity.This is a well known fact.

The Circle has no beginning, no end and no direction. Because of these attributes, The Circle represents completeness that outweighs space and time to infinite.Being a symbol of Divinity. It also is well known as a

Symbol of Divinity it is also a Symbol of perfection, completeness and unity.

"Meditation and Prayer are the *Gnosis* (insight, intuition, imagination and Wisdom) through which we know and feel that we are part of

something more magical and Divine than our simple material "shelves";

that Divinity resides in us by way of our Atman; that we are

expansive spiritual beings; and that we can improve and perfect

ourselves, to any degree we desire, by way of the Spiritual,

un-measurable and infinite Powers which reside within us."(Joe Panek,from the article,A Seeker's Thoughts 2010)

As far as my personal beliefs,the pentacle represents the morning star(also a name for Jesus)It also was the star of Bethlehem that announced the birth of Jesus,it is in the celestial plane as a beacon in the night.

This metaphor as a beacon, a light in the darkness is very closely related to all that Jesus is to the believer.

Considering the elements that are both represented within life and within us as humans,I see them like this:Here are five elements, four of matter (earth, air, fire and water) and THE quintessential - spirit. These may be arrayed around the pentagrams points.

The word quintessential derives from this fifth element - the spirit. Tracing a path around the pentagram, the elements are placed in order of density - spirit (or aether). fire, air, water, earth. Earth and fire are basal, fixed; air and water are free, flowing.

Spirit: The most important of the elements,in my theory.Spirit is what we should seek in all our endeavors.It keeps everything in perfect balance,

When the superior point of the Pentagram is pointing up, it represents Divinity.

Earth represents the dust we are made from,also our spiritual body.This denotes the scripture "As on earth,as it is in Heaven"also relates to "As Above,So Below"

In Wiccan belief.This element reminds us we are grounded and rooted in faith,Just as a tree uses it's root system.Earth is the principle of solidity and reflects the metaphysical principle of Law.

Air:Is our breath,Breath in the Hebrew means Spirit.The same spirit that was breathed into the first of Creation at the beginning of time itself.

Oxygen gives life to its host,without it we would die.Represents our creativity.It is the element of intellect;reflects the metaphysical principle of Life.

Fire:The fire of the Holy spirit,our passion,what drives us.It is a well known fact,fire was the first gift given to mankind.

Fire represents courage.As the old saying goes,you must pass threw the fire to get threw to the other end(our trials)It is a purifier.

Fire is the element of action and reflects the metaphysical Light.

Water:The human body is mostly made up of this element,it makes up our blood,it is within the tears we cry in any emotion be it joy or sadness.It is what encompasses our intuition and emotions.

It is the element of fertility,reflecting the metaphysical law of Love.

 The spark of Life descending from God, the divine source of life to the simplest embryonic form (earth), rising to flow (water - air) on our plane of existence (compare with the intonation of the AUM mantra), then again descending to the fire of purification before again rising as a divine spark to find again his spiritual source.

The pentagram tells us that we have the ability to bring Spirit to Earth.

Without these vital elements that also make up the universe and it's survival.Nothing could thrive or live without the other:all is balance,if one elements is lacking the rest suffer also.

Without the heat,light of the sun earth would freeze,without the rain the crops would die and wither:as would mammals.

Without the dust,which is also what our human bodies are made up of,there would be a void of everything.

Without oxygen we could not breath,the trees would not exist to give off the oxygen...if any of the other elements were missing.

Most importantly without Spirit,we would be as robots walking without purpose.There would be no love,hope,faith.The universe would not exist,Spirit is the intangible,everlasting,infinite factor that is not only the heartbeat of the world but within ourselves.

"To the followers of Pythagoras, it was called "The Pentalpha" being composed of five interlaced A's or Alphas. The Alpha being the first word of the alphabet, we can perhaps view it as showing forth unity in the midst of multiplicity. The individual as part of the Whole.

The Blazing Pentagram, the Flaming Star, the sign of Divine omnipotence, the ineffable symbol of the Verb made flesh, the terrific star of the Magi, is also named Pentalpha because it contains in itself five Alphas, that is to say five letters "A" within its five angles.

PENTA = Signifies Five in Greek.

ALPHA = First letter of the Greek Alphabet.

GRAMMA = Graphic or Letter in Greek.

Around the Pentalpha we find the word TETRAGRAMMATON.

TETRA = Signifies four in Greek.

GRAMMA = Signifies Graphic or Letter in Greek.

TON = In the Greek language at the end of any word, denotes the union of two, three, four, five or more unities or letters in one single name or unity.

Therefore TETRAGRAMMATON is the magic word or Greek "mantra" of an immense priesthood power that synthesizes in one unity the four Kabbalistics letters (הוהי Iod, He Vau, He) that in kabbalah are utilized to name divinity.

From right to left is written IOD, HEI, VAU, HEI, these are pronounced JEHOVAH or better said, IOD - HAVAH. The LUNI-SOLAR Androgen, the FATHER-MOTHER, our interior, particular individual MONAD.

From right to left is written מדא ALEPH, DALETH, MEM, these are pronounced ADAM, the HUM-MANAS or Celestial Man made in the image and likeness of God.

From right to left is written PE, CHET, DALETH, these are pronounced PEHAD, which means awe, ardor; synonym of the other Hebrew word, הארי reverence and profound respect towards "SHADDAI EL CHAI" the essence of God (The Ens Seminis). The beginning of wisdom is the ardor, awe (דחפ or הארי) of Jehovah.- Proverb 9: 10

From right to left is written רפכ KAPH, PHE, REISH, these are pronounced KAPHAR which means expiation; that is to say, to die in oneself and to make supreme sacrifices in order to expiate or to pay our karmic debts.

The letter A "Alpha" is the first letter of the Greek alphabet. It is located beneath the eyes and form its mouth; it symbolizes the Verb or Word, the principle of creation.

"In the beginning was the Word, and the Word was with God and the Word was God".

The letter ☐ ◆ "Omega" is situated between the legs and opens inward and upward.

It is the last letter of the Greek alphabet, and symbolizes the Cosmic Christ or Universal Verb, the Prana, that when transformed by the metabolism of the body, finally remains deposited in potency, within the Ens Seminis, as Christ in substance.

The Internal Christ is the Alpha A and the Omega ☐, the beginning and the ending, that is, was and shall be. The ending is equal to the beginning plus the experience of the cycle."

(The above is a detailed desciption of an Esoteric Pentagram)

The Cross

A Celtic cross is a symbol that combines a cross with a ring surrounding the intersection.

The symbol is associated with Celtic Christianity, although it has older, pre-Christian origins. Such crosses form a major part of Celtic art.

A standing Celtic cross, made of stone and often richly ornamented, is called a high cross or Irish Cross. Celtic crosses may have had origins in the early Coptic church.

The Cross was originally a pagan symbol in countless belief systems from Native American Spirituality, to Celtic Crosses What these crosses mean to us today and what they meant when Christianity was new to Celtic Britain and Ireland are in some ways the same and in some ways different. The cross either vertical or diagonal with equal length arms is a universal

mark. It is so primal that it exists in all cultures as does the circle.

These marks are opposites. The circle contains and is unending while the cross both reaches out and marks a specific, finite point at the center.

A plain circle is often a symbol for the moon and a circle with a cross within or the arms of a cross without are universal symbols for the sun.

The cross by itself relates to other ideas. The four directions or the four corners of the Earth, the vertical and the horizontal coming together imply the joining of forces such as Heaven and Earth.

The symbol of Celtic Christianity,is the Celtic cross.It is derived from the ancient Roman monogram of Christ,made from the Greek letters *chi* and *rho*.

This form of cross with it's outstetched arms and enclosing circle,is derived from an ancient from dating back thousands of years before Christianity.It is an ancient symbol of the sun.

The placement of the crosses at the crossroads and also marketplaces,mimicked the same placement as the pagan monuments.Many monastaries were build over pagan temples during this time.

The Celtic solar calendar of ancient times,was made up of two solstices,two equinoxes,and four cross-quarter days marking the seasons.The four solarfestivals,marked on a round representing the path of the year,form a solar cross,the basis of the Celtic cross.

As a symbol of spirituality,the Ionic cross represented the crossoad of life and death joined together with the eternal circle of Heaven.From a pagan's prospective it represented the coming together of male and female

symbolism.The four arms also were seen as the calendar of the zodiac,important to early Christians.The four cardinal directions,along with the four fixed signs of the zodiac were representations of Matthew(along with his emblem,an angel),Mark(the lion)Luke(the ox),and John(the eagle),Christ was represented by the center solar disk.

The Triquetra

Derived from the Latin word,("three cornered")made up of the three interlocked *versica pisces* symbols(fish shaped symbols)marking where three circles intersect.

This symbol is related to the ancient Neolithic and early Christian mother goddesses,the emblem probably represented the intertwined domains of earth,ocean,and sky.

In time this was adopted for Christian use representing Father,Son and Holy Ghost.

The triquetra was used in 1611 as the logo of the King James Bible.

This symbol for pagans represents the female aspects of the Trinity.

Wheel

WHEEL: A universal symbol of or cosmic unity, astrology, "the circle of life," evolution, etc. The pagan sacred circle plus any number of radiating spokes or petals form the wheel - a Wheel of Life to Buddhists, a Medicine Wheel to Native Americans, a Mandala to Hindus.

It symbolizes unity, movement, the sun, the zodiac, reincarnation, and earth's cycles of renewal. Pagans use it in astrology, magic and many kinds of rituals. (See Medicine Wheel and Quartered Circle)

This SUN WHEEL became a magical amulet to the Celtic Gauls or Gaels in Europe. Later, "Christians adopted the form, changing it slightly, so that it became a Christ monogram drawn within a circle."

Yin Yang, Tao

A Chinese Tao picture of universal harmony and the unity between complimentary opposites: light/dark, male/female, etc.

Yin is the dark, passive, negative female principle. Yang is the light, active, positive principle.

Since the holistic balance between Yin and Yang is dynamic and constantly changing, it illustrates the consensus process, the vision of global unity, and the blending of opposing energies at the heart of Holistic Health.

Since it represent monism (all is one) and pantheism (all is God), it opposes Christianity, which shows us that there is only one God (monotheism), and only in Christ can we be one.

Fish: the fish -- ever-watchful with its unblinking eyes -- was one of the most important symbols of Christ to the early Christians.

In Greek, the phrase, "Jesus Christ, Son of God Savior," is "Iesous Christos Theou Yios Soter."

The first letters of each of these Greek words, when put together, spell "ichthys," the Greek word for "fish" (ICQUS).

This symbol can be seen in the Sacraments Chapel of the Catacombs of St. Callistus. Because of the story of the miracle of the loaves and fishes, the fish symbolized, too, the Eucharist

Phoenix: The Phoenix is a mythical creature said to build a nest when old, and set it on fire. It would then rise from the ashes in victory.

Because of these myths (believed by the Egyptians, Greeks, and Orientals), the bird came to symbolize Christ.

St. Brigid's Cross: St. Brigid fashioned a Cross out of rushes as she sat near a dying chieftan's bed.

He asked her about what she was doing and in explaining, she recounted the story of Christ, whereupon the chieftan converted. Catholics -- especially Irish Catholics -- fashion Crosses like these on the Feast of St. Brigid (1 February).

Triade

This ancient symbol was found in the Neolithic era.Found on ancient tombs,believed to be connected with the sun and rebirth.

The Triade, Triskele, or Triple Spiral, is an ancient Celtic symbol related to earthly life, the afterlife and reincarnation.

It is drawn in one continuous line, suggesting a fluid movement of time. Triades are one of the most common elements of Celtic art. They are found in a variety of styles in both ancient and contemporary uses, especially in relation to depictions of the Mother Goddess.

They also evoke the universal concept of the domains of material existence- earth, water, and sky; body, mind and spirit; and the eternally spiraling cycles of time.

Used in a personal spiritual practice, this symbol reinforces the movement and interconnection between the dimensions or realms of consciousness – ordinary reality, the underworld, the overworld, all integral to a complete earth experience.

In larger context, the Triade radiates the potential of complete experience and wisdom for all.

In water, the harmonic convergence of all truths bring a quality to water that nourishes all cells with expansive potential for greater creation.

Ankh

Egyptian cross symbolizing a mythical eternal life, rebirth, and the life-giving power of the sun.

The ankh representing life after death, eternal immortality. It was a symbol of life everlasting. Also, known as Nem Ankh, the key of life, it later entered Christian iconography as the crux ansata, the

handled or "eyed" cross.

The ankh is typically associated with material things such as water (which was believed by Egyptians to regenerate life;

symbol for water), air, or the sun, as well as with the gods, who are frequently pictured carrying an ankh. The Egyptian king is often associated with the ankh, either in possession of an ankh (providing life to his people) or being given an ankh (or stream of ankhs) by the gods. It was thought to contain (*"the breath of life"*).

Anthropomorphic pictures of the ankh sometimes show it holding an ostrich-feather fan behind the pharaoh in a variant form of this idea. Similarly, chains of ankhs were shown poured out of water vessels over the king as a symbol of the regenerating power of water.

Libation vessels which held the water used in religious ceremonies were themselves sometimes produced in the shape of the ankh hieroglyph.

Awen

A Welsh bard Iolo Morganwg, printing this emblem in his book of druid philosophy in the eighteenth century.

The three parts represent the domains of earth, sea and sky, as well as opposites in harmony. The left and right rays represent the balance of feminine and masculine energies, darkness and light, negative and positive and so on in complete balance and harmony.

Also a symbol pronouncing love, wisdom and truth. It is also said that the Awen stands for not simply inspiration, but for inspiration of truth; without Awen one cannot proclaim truth.

The three foundations of Awen are the understanding of truth, the love of truth, and the maintaining of truth.

This symbol represents the divine illumination sought after by the seekers on the druid path.

Awen is a welsh word poetically translated as 'sacred inspiration'. Literally it means 'flowing spirit'. It is the essence of life, the creative energy which flows through the universe.

According to the Order of Bards, Ovates and Druids (OBOD)describe the three lines as rays emanating from three points of light, with those points representing the triple aspect of deity and, also, the points at which the sun rises on the equinoxes and solstices - known as the Triad of the Sunrises.

The emblem as used by the OBOD is surrounded by three circles representing the three circles of creation.

A Look Back In Time

I have always been a firm believer,if you want to know the acurate fact on any subject,you must search for yourself.Taking the word of others sometimes proves nothing.

The information they gather, could have been word of mouth through others who gave a short answer, without researching anything.

Time has a way of rewriting history.It is almost similar to the concept of gossiping,a story starts out very different than the final outcome.Things are added to and taken away from the original facts.

Earlier in my life,I attended various denominations.I even taught Sunday school at an Assembly Of God.

Through my journey at this time I came upon some, that would worry about every small thing they did in a day may or may not be a sin.

In their mind it was if,God would surely be mad at them or they let the Creator down in some way.

Strange how people think they are turning people to Christianity with a lesson of fear and condemnation.

I searched within myself,I knew that there had to be more out there than the same messages I was hearing,I dared not question them for myself.To question is not wrong in the Creator's eyes.

I think it is part of the growing process otherwise we are believing what others are telling us their concept of spirit is and what it is not.

To the church organization to question anything,or to go to any source outside of the Bible is considered wrong.

I still read my books. I still found the same idea of the message the Bible had in other sources,even within the daily walks I saw spirit in everything.It was nice to come to understand that spirit was in more places than only behind the church doors.It was within me.It was within the seeds that became a flower.

It was within the sacred space of the fields and trees outside,nature within itself is sacred..an extention of divinity,(life).I too was in the process of being planted.

I knew a seed had to be planted within the earth,receiving the proper light and water in order to grow and bloom.

After all light and water as a metaphor for spirit doesn't have a specific one place it can be..all plants grow from the same everywhere.There are many species of flowers yet they are still considered a flower,no matter what color or height.

It seemed to me that many of the churches expected all individuals to be the same,to believe the same and become numb to the power that is within.Only to hear their own concepts of Deity never questioning the laws that define we as humans.

To accept the fact that we are sinful that's that.That we should live in constant fear of God and the devil?As far as I had come to understand,our concept of Deity was not a spirit of fear,but of love,power and a sound mind.

To experience the power within is similar to seeing colors in a new and crisp way,tasting in a heightened manner,and hearing song beneath the mundane world.

Senses are heightened,there is a peace,a rush of a spiral of understanding that you are a spiritual individual,given the wisdom to seek treasures that lie hidden within your own heart.

They do not lie waiting anywhere else.It is the knowing that you are alive,and relishing in that knowing.

I have heard a theory that makes perfect example of the personality of Diety;The Bible says God is a spirit (John 4:24). It also says that the spirit, given by God, is what gives man understanding (Job 32:8).

And finally, it says that God is light (I John 1:5).

Considering light, it is energy. We are created with the same physical and spiritual attributes of this energy, or light. Everything that exists in the universe is made up of energy.

Every atom has electrons, sub-atomic particles containing an electrical charge, which orbit around the atom's nucleus. Every atom has energy.

There is a scientific law that states that energy cannot be created or destroyed, it simply changes form (conservation of energy). All the energy that ever existed, that was present at the beginning, still exists. This is a great description of Deity. Simply energy.

Many forms of energy cannot be seen. Everything is sacred, because everything is made from the energy that is God.

Albert Einstein once stated, "Energy cannot be created or destroyed, it can only be changed from one form to another."

If energy cannot be created or destroyed, we can safely assume two things:

Energy always existed.

Energy will always continue to exist.

This means that energy is essentially eternal.

The Law Of Attraction is a universal law. It is neutral to religion and creed.

The same way you throw an apple in the air and it falls back down due to the Law of Gravity, the Law of Attraction will allow you to create your reality for yourself through the use of your thoughts.

We can assume then,with everything that is energy including the universe,we as humans, must have the same ability to harness that energy sending this invisible force throughout the world,creating healing and peace.

Such as the theory that one butterfly moving it's wings on one continent can create a reaction on another.This is known as a ripple effect,simple energy forms of thought,prayer and meditation can create change.

If we start with ourselves as that change,searching for ourselves on the meaning of life.Choosing for ourselves what we view about the world,we become free.Freedom is the beginning of breaking the chains of society norms in order to live a more abundant life.

If we continue to use the keys we carry to unlock our own doors to the questions we seek,we reach this freedom.It is our own and no one can steal it from us.

Consider how a thought put into action,or told to others creates an idea that is either positive or negative.

What starts as a small spark turns into an inferno.This is relative to the case of how some in society view witches.It all originated from some thought stretched into something that it was clearly not.

King James I of England held much legal influence of the witch-hunts of the late 1500s.

He greatly feared the power of witches. He believed wholly that a storm which threatened to sink his ship and drown both him and his 15-year-old wife, Queen Anne, was summoned by witches.

As a result of this belief, the two women "responsible" were burned at the stake (one still alive at the time).James I was notorious for being paranoid about witches, spells, and so on. This was, in part, due to volatile politics of the time. The scripture "thou shall not suffer a witch to live"Lev 20:27 was taken out of context translated the word chasaph--which is Hebrew for poisoner-- to mean "witch" instead

The real Biblical passage was about the disturbing crime of poisoning in the Jewish community.

When that line was originally written, poisonings were a growing concern. And, in that "eye for an eye" era, the logical sentence for a poisoner was death.

"Witch" is not specific to any one religion. It's merely a label for a person who practices the Science of Energy Manipulation. The main belief is that of love, healing and never harming another. In a sense is this not the same message that Jesus came with?

"Witches have long been feared and hated in Christian circles. Even today, pagans and Wiccans remain a target of Christian persecution — especially in America.

It seems that they long ago took on an identity which reached far beyond their own existence and became a symbol for Christians — but a symbol of what? Maybe an examination of the events will give us some clues.

As the Inquisition proceeded merrily along through the 1400s, its focus shifted from Jews and heretics and moved towards so-called witches. Although Pope Gregory IX had authorized the killing of witches back in the 1200s, the fad just didn't catch on for while. In 1484, Pope Innocent VIII issued a bull declaring that witches did indeed exist, and thus it became a heresy to believe otherwise.

This was quite a reversal, because in 906 the Canon Episocopi, a church law, declared that belief in the existence and operation of witchcraft was heresy.

As a result of this, church authorities tortured and killed thousands of women, and not a few men, in an effort to get them to confess that they flew through the sky, had sexual relations with demons, turned into animals, and engaged in various sorts of black magic.

The creation of the concept of devil-worship, followed by its persecution, allowed the church to more easily subordinate people to authoritarian control and openly denigrate women.

Most of what was passed off as witchcraft were simply fictional creations of the church, but some of it was genuine or almost-genuine practices of pagans and wiccans.

In fact, the word "witch" from the Old English word "wicca," which was applied to male and female members of an ancient pagan tradition which reveres masculine, feminine and earthly aspects of God. Wiccan tradition involved both heaven and earth, both the next world and this world.

It also involved a tradition which was not quite as hierarchical and authoritarian, and this represented a direct challenge to the Christian church.

The additional persecution of anything which resembled feminine religiosity went to interesting lengths in that devotion to Mary became suspect.

Today the figure of Mary is both popular and important in the Catholic church, but to the Inquisition it was a possible sign of overemphasizing the feminine aspect of Christianity.

In the Canary Islands, Aldonca de Vargas was reported to the Inquisition for nothing more than smiling at hearing mention of Mary.

The subservience of women to men was a common theme in early Christian writings — an outgrowth of both traditional patriarchal attitudes and the extreme hierarchical nature of the church itself.

Groups which did not hold to hierarchy in any form were attacked immediately. There is no shared authority between the genders in traditional Christianity, either in the church or in the home.

Homosexuality would be particularly threatening to this ideology, as it raises the potential of redefining gender roles, especially in the home.

Witness how the recent attacks upon homosexuality in society has progressed hand-in-hand with the mindless promotion of vague "traditional family values," particularly those which "put women in their place" and reinforce male dominance in the home.

With a married couple of two women or two men, who exactly is supposed to be in charge and who meekly obedient?

Never mind that the Christians who fear such relationships will never be asked to make those decisions themselves — the mere fact that people are making such decisions on their own rather than obeying someone else's religious proclamations is quite enough to give them fits of apoplexy."(Witches, Women, and

Witchcraft History and Background By
Austin Cline,2011

Appalachian Granny Magick

"Appalachian Granny Magic is only recently being heard of by many people even though the tradition is very old, dating all the way back to the first settlers of the Appalachian Mountains. In the 1700's immigrants came and brought along their Irish and Scottish traditions.

Those two traditions were then blended with the local traditions of the Cherokee Indians. Although it has been around for a long time there is very little information written about it.

It is known to be an earth based tradition passed on by Scottish, Irish and Cherokee ancestors. It is the belief that nature is sacred. The Appalachian Witch respects and reveres nature however they do not worship it.

Appalachian Granny Magic was passed on from parents to their children for many generations and usually was not passed outside of the family.

The Appalachian communities were small, rural and secluded, so the customs, wisdom, and practices were not as often lost, forgotten, or modernized. Because of this many of the ancient Irish or Scottish songs, rhymes, dances, spells, rituals and 'The Craft,' were more accurately preserved in Appalachia than in most other places in the world. Many of the Scot/Irish traditions, as well as the Cherokee traditions, have been carried on in Appalachia up to this day.

In the secluded mountains of the South Eastern United States, this form of Witchcraft continued right on through the decades of the eighteenth, nineteenth, and the twentieth centuries; a time when Witchcraft was being forgotten and abandoned by the world.

The people of the mountains still relied upon Mother Nature.

The fertility of the crops, the livestock, and of the people themselves was as important to the Appalachians of the 1900's as it was to the immigrants in the 1600's. Mother Nature, Jack Frost, Father Winter and other deities continued in the Appalachian region, as a part of the people's beliefs.

Most Appalachian Witches believe that all people have a spirit; that all things of the earth have a spirit. They believe that spirits are a part of nature but not a part of the energy of god; they do not believe in many gods and goddesses as separate entities, they believe in one universal GOD.

Appalachian Witches observe the sabbats, solstices and equinoxes, but do not relate them to mythology; it is the seasonal changes that they recognize.

The terms 'Witch,' Witchcraft', 'spells' and 'charms' never became taboo in Appalachia; nearly every mountain top and holler had their 'Witch'; although practitioners usually called themselves cunning or wise women.

Local folk went to the wise ones for prophecy, and protection, for delivering babies, healing with herbs, and other remedies and cures; providing abortions, love potions, and poisons; divination and casting of curses and blessings, or care for the dying.

Often a mountain community had no doctor to call, the Witches were the only healers available to them, well into the twentieth century. (The local 'Witch' was also called upon to dowse for water.)

Fairy and leprechaun lore was brought by the Scots and Irish to Appalachia and the Witches continued to believe in them.

The Cherokee people had their own magical beings when the Scots and Irish arrived. Offerings are still given to little people in Appalachia; it is as simple as leaving a bowl of milk on the door step or throwing a piece of cornbread out a window for them.

Working with spirits of the dead and ancestral spirit guide workings were also passed down, these practices trace back to Scotland, Ireland and the Cherokee Nation.

Spirits were shown respect; believed to be those who passed before… ancestors, family; but not all spirits are believed to be helpful, some can be troublesome. 'Haints' are feared spirits; spells, charms, and rituals are practiced to keep them away.

One of the most common 'haint' related spells requires that the porch ceiling of a home be painted 'haint' blue.

This is believed to keep the 'haints' out of the home.

Divination is popular in Appalachia. Many of the Witches read Tarot, and regular playing cards, tea leaves, coffee grounds, spider webs and clouds. Scrying in water, dirt, or sand is common.

The Appalachian Witch tools are different from 'Wiccan' tools. The Wand, is called the 'rod', it is the dowsing rod and for some Witches the most important tool.

It is usually a long straight rod, made of wood from a flowering tree such as dogwood, apple or peach for Water dowsing.

A ritual blade is not used; a kitchen knife or an ax will be used instead.

Cauldrons are used for many purposes. A cauldron placed in the front yard was an 'open-for-business' Witches' sign in times gone by.

Mirrors, candles, brooms, pottery, and baskets are other common tools and some of those items are still made at home, by hand in the mountains of Appalachia.

Many times the only tools used are the mind and willpower of the Witch.

Appalachian magic was a solitary practice. It required little preparation and no expensive tools or specialized knowledge.

It was very practical and down-to-earth; eclectic and informal in its approach, rather than 'High' or 'Ritualistic' in nature.

It was primarily concerned with omens, curses, cures, and protection. Ritual clothing was generally not used, and circles were not cast. All nature was believed to be sacred, so a "sacred" place did not have to be created; Appalachian witches believe magic need not be ritualistic to be effective because Magic is essentially prayer.

SOME modern Appalachian Witches, being eclectic already with Scottish, Irish, and Cherokee roots, have started to use some other traditions practices such as wearing ritual clothing and casting a circle.

Here is a sample of spells, remedies and beliefs of the people in the Appalachian Mountains.

If you dream of a birth, there will be a death and vice versa.

If your ears are burning, someone is talking about you.

When a certain area of your body itches, it foretells of things to come:

left eye = you will be made happy

right eye = you will be made angry

palm in general = you will receive money

back of hand in general = you will give away money

fingers in general = you will receive money only to spend it quickly

right palm = you will shake hands with a stranger

left palm = you will touch money

souls of feet = you will walk on strange grounds

A horseshoe aimed upward, nailed to a barn or house, will protect from evil and bad luck.

If a bird flies into the house it is bad luck. Finding a dead bird is also considered a bad omen.

Dried basil hung over the doorways, windows, fireplaces will keep 'haints' from entering.

Garlic placed under a pillow or knocking 3 times on the bed post will prevent nightmares caused by spirits.

Knocking 3 times beside your door before entering deters 'haints'.

Bells and chimes are methods of keeping 'haints' away. (windchimes)

If you feel you are being followed by a 'haint', cross over running water. "Haints' cannot cross over running water.

To turn away negative forces from humans or animals toss nine broom straws, one at a time, on a fire at sunset.

Squeaky doors are invitations to 'haints'.

Windows can be protected from 'haints' with sprigs of fresh rosemary and basil.

Placing a fern or ivy on the porch will protect against curses. If it's eaten by an animal, then a curse is already in place.

Yarrow or Lichen Moss hung on a crib will drive away curses or drive a nail into the crib post.

Carrying a piece from a tree that has been struck by lightening will protect the carrier.

Acorns thrown on the roof before it rains will prevent hail damage.

Oak logs burned in the hearth will protect the home.

Pine and Cedar logs burned in the hearth brings prosperity

Birch logs burned in the hearth brings happiness

Elm protects against curses and evil.

Basil and Rosemary tossed into a fire protects and brings happiness.

A white dove flying over your house is an omen that there will be a marriage, some believe it is generally a good omen.

To rid your self of a wart, cut a potato in half and rub on the wart.

To make your hair grow you should place clippings under the down spout of your home.

To cure a child of asthma, have the child cut a mark on a tree as high up as can be reached.

When the child is taller than the mark on the tree the asthma will be gone.

If someone plants a cedar he will die when it grows large enough to shade his coffin."(Firewytch, March 07 2007)

Painting your front porch blue,keeps negativity away.

Hanging a broom above your door,keeps unwanted company out.

If a broom falls,company is one the way.

If your nose itches,someone is talking behind your back.Plant rosemary beside your door or gateway for luck.

If you find a lady bug in your house it is considered good luck.

Never kill a spider in your home,they bring good fortune.

Twist an apple's stem ans say the alphabet,where ever it stops is the initial of who you are to marry.

The cemetery is considered the city of the dead,they know when you are there and welcome you.

Strangely my grandmother taught me,and these 'old wives tales'I suppose it is true when you search long enough you will find.I just found the definition I believe of my heritage.

Other insights she bestowed on me at a very young age,were ones concerning what happens when we die.The spirit leaves the body and goes on.

Our body is simply a shell as that of a turtle or a crysillis. Spirit is eternal and neverending.

Spiritual Housecleaning

It is important to clean your house for health reasons, but also for the purpose of getting rid of negative energies that may settle there.

Lemon was often used for it's scent and it's ability to lift the spirits of the owner.

Lavender was put beside the window or on the bed linen to promote sleep and tranquility. It's purpose placed in a window sill was to ward of uninvited bugs.

Sage has historically been used in smudging rituals as a means of invoking purification, protection, longevity, and immortality.

The burning of sage is a popular practice espoused by various healing and spiritual groups. The word sage - salvia - comes from the Latin word salvare, which translated means "To heal".

The ritual of smudging can be defined as "spiritual house cleaning." Smudging is the common name given to the Sacred Smoke Bowl Blessing, a powerful cleansing technique from the Native American tradition.

However the burning of herbs for emotional, psychic, and spiritual purification is common practice in many religious, healing, and spiritual traditions.

The smoke attaches itself to negative energy. As the smoke clears it takes the negative energy with it, releasing it to regenerate into something more positive.

Tests have also shown that the smoke of burning sage literally changes the ionization polarity of the air. Sandlewood also is used for this purpose.

A bowl of salt will work just as well to disperse the negative energy.

Another way of cleaning house is to do just precisely that. Going from the top down and from the back to the front, always working toward the doors, clean out your living space.

Dust, straighten, wash the walls, and while you are doing this, also focus your activities with the intent of cleaning more than just the physical aspect of the house. As you wipe away dirt from the walls, reach out on the level of the subtle reality and also scrape away any negative energies that have built up.

As you clean out the cramped closets and back hidey holes, throwing away the worn out junk you don't really need anymore, try also to mentally throw out any old ideas, attitudes, or habits that you also don't really need to keep around any more.

Consecrate the water you clean your house with beforehand, and dump the energy you want to disperse into your bucket of cleaning water as you go.

Open the front door and sweep out the dust and refuse, focusing on the broom so it sweeps away more than just physical dirt. Finish up by burning incense in every room and fuming the living space so it smells clean and fresh.

One of the most important aspects of spiritual protection is "white light" protection. It's very simple to do, and maybe you've even read about it or done it without knowing it. It's very effective at removing and preventing negative energy from harming you.

To do this, just visualize an egg-shaped sphere of brilliant white light completely surrounding you, from head to toe.

Really focus on seeing it clearly in your mind, and keep building it up so it's SUPER bright and glowing. See it as a solid barrier of protection that negativity cannot cross.

If you wish, you can also say a prayer of protection while doing this.

You don't have to get fancy with the wording. Say something like, "God/dess, please surround me with a sphere of powerful, brilliant white light.

Send the Archangels to protect me from all harm, and please send my Spirit Guides to guide me, guard me and keep away all negative influences.

You can do this for yourself, loved ones, pets, even your house.

Here is a list of common plants and herbs that are very good for removing (and preventing) negative energy: aloe, anise, barley, basil, bay leaf, cactus, carnation, cedar, chamomile, cinnamon, clove, cumin, curry, dill, dragon's blood, eucalyptus, fennel, fern, flax, frankincense, garlic, ginseng, ivy, lavendar, myrrh, onion, parsley, pepper, peppermint, rosemary, sage, thyme, violet.

White candles are also great for removing negative energy, and you can make them work even better by "charging" them. (in fact, you can charge your herbs the same way to help activate their natural properties) To "charge" something means that you are infusing it with energy, and your intention.

Rub olive oil above your doors and windows and simply say a prayer and bless your house,this can also be used on people or animals to heal and cleanse.

It is also important to keep good hygiene,sea salts used in a bath,or certain herbs cleanse away the daily negativity that 'settles'on us.

It is amazing how our spirits are often bogged down by this,from others,situations or just having a bad day.

Dust in mostly made up of human skin,which carried with it energies of that person.

This and other spiritual energies settle on us.Ever felt depressed,nervous or out of sorts after someone with a bad attitude visits this is a example of being zapped of your own energy.

Since all things are made up of energy emotions too,they can effect other people.

So,when I refer to "house" cleaning I am referring to your physical living space as well as your physical body,mind,emotions and spirit.

Creating Sacred Space, Archangels

Just as in a Christian church, a form of prayer circle is formed when performing a ritual(rit·u·al)

By definition:

A religious or solemn ceremony consisting of a series of actions performed according to a prescribed order

- the ancient rituals of Christian worship

- the role of ritual in religion

- observance of set forms in public worship.

Unfortunately this term has been taken out of context many times, by those who let their imagination and the stigma that is now attached to this word run away with them.

A ritual simply is just that, like any other prayer service, when more than one individual is gathered to give thanks for their blessings, observe the wheel of the year, new moons ect.

Around ten years ago,when I merged into the pagan community,I would hesitate to speak of this word to my Christian friends.

I am sure that the media has never helped this quest,of taking the false beliefs out of paganism.I would get question such as do you preform animal sacrifices,is this devil worship..things of this nature.

My answer"no",and "no" It is such a twist of the true facts.

No animals are harmed,in fact not even there."would you take one to church?"I am sure in the ancient days,even in the bible people no matter what label of religion,were guilty of these thing.

For me and others I know..this would be like killing your mascot so to speak.

In Shamanism animal guides are the same to us as guardian angels,meaning different things,teaching lessons in spirit.

We revere all living things,to kill one would be like killing a part of ourselves.In our spiritual quest these are important,in meditation animal guides often come to speak lessons of wisdom.

I am sure the Creator uses these as an example,just as in parables.The simple things have meaning,can pass on symbols of courage,faith and protection.This is the basis of paganism,a earth-centered religion.

We see it as an extent of God/Goddess..just as everything in the universe is connected and all things have spirit.

From the dust in the universe,to the rocks,trees,animals we are all connected.

Just as the branches of a mighty oak.The roots are where we have came from,symbolize being grounded in faith,the trunk is Diety,the branches are "Us" reaching above to the Heavens to gain insight and knowledge.

There are many leaves on the tree,this could symbolize the different walks of life,of denomination,faith,how each sees the Eternal.

As far as being devil worship,defiantly not.Casting circle we smudge with sage,or water/salt to keep all negative energy and thoughts away.The main principle is one of love and communion with the Divine as well as nature.

As far as I understand from within,all things must be balanced.This applies to everything in life,also in spirit.Like a scale too much positive or negative will tip it..the balance of the two for the well being of self and others is the key.

The scientific laws of nature also exhibit balance.Too much of a good rain will cause a flood,too much sun promotes a drought.

I am so glad everything works this way in perfect unison and harmony.

After the circle of protection is cast,the elements are called in with the directions,four winds of spirit.

This practice is based upon the text of Isaiah 11:1-3 where the Four Winds or Spirit of God is spoken of: The Spirit of Yahweh; The Spirit of Wisdom and Understanding; The Spirit of Counsel & Might; The Spirit of Knowledge and Seeing.

Raphael

As a solitary,I use East as my first because this is where the sun rises; new beginnings,rebirth,Illumination, birth, initiation.bringing the truth of illumination to our path.East represents the element of air.

East represents the Spirit of God, the Archangel Raphael, the element of Air and the Nature of Healing.

This can be three aspects: physically, emotionally or spiritually. Raphael literally means the "healing power of God." We are seeking to restore balance in our lives, wholeness, and the restoring of the unity of being.

The fish Raphael carries is an ancient symbol

of medicine. Raphael is also called the Angel of Science and Knowledge.

Grounded in the nature of spirit and in the nature of matter, in and through your body, here and now in this earthly reality.

.Raphael is Regent, or Angel of the Sun.

A common practice is also to take a fresh glass of water, asking Raphael to bless this water with the qualities of the Rising Sun and of healing properties for mind, body, and spirit, taking that power into oneself as one drinks. This is a good practice for self-healing.

Raphael is also considered the angelic presence behind the physical sun that illuminates our solar system.

Uriel

Then North. The Element of Earth. The Spirit or Wind of Knowledge and Seeing the Divine One.

This is the Direction of Embodiment and Manifestation, This knowledge is within and all around us. By entering into the energy of Uriel we come to see differently, as if we see in and behind all things as to the truth of their nature.

Uriel means the Light of God, and it is this Light that brings illumination. This illumination then needs to become embodied and manifested on Earth.

We all have moments of deep insight, experiences of the Sacred One in one form or another, whether it be the sacredness of this earth, a depth of understanding about our journey, or a direct experience of the Light.

Whatever our experiences it is essential to integrate and embody them, so that true change occurs in our lives, and not simply knowing it as a moment out of time and space.

Also North is the direction of our ancestors

Gabriel

Then turning west, recognizing Gabriel; a teacher and a messenger of truth. Archangel Gabriel,is angel of the Incarnation and of Consolation, warrior.

Gabriel ("God is my strength")His (sometimes her) name means God is my Strength - Associated with the Water Element.

Guidance in your spiritual life , Revelation of your life plan and purpose, Release Joy, Happiness, and Fulfillment, Dissolution of discouragement, Help establish Discipline and Order in your life.

Michael

Turning to the South, the Element of Fire, The Spirit or Wind of Counsel and Might.

The name Michael means "Who is like unto God," therefore Michael is the guardian angel of humanity.Part of Michael's job is the act of purification.

In essence, we are asking to be purified of that which no longer serves us.

We are asking for the power and courage to come into the place of our will of righteousness, that is, the will of right action and/or right wisdom or wiseness.

We are seeking to be liberated from all that is not right action or right wisdom in our lives.

Fire represents our passion,creation and inspiration.

Then the sacred space has been created,focusing our intent and energy in this one space that is now considered holy ground,free of negativity.

Asking for the things in our lives that need to be changed,praying for peace,sending healing energy to the world,honoring Diety,being thankful for the harvest in our life.

I recently ran across a beautiful Native American method for creating sacred prayer space,or casting circle:

"Oh Spirit of the East, Land of the rising Sun, Of Air, the winds that blow across the lands. Of new beginnings each day. and of open horizons.

We ask for your wisdom and blessing here with us today. Please join us, Spirit of the East."

"Oh Spirit of the South, Place of Passion, Fire and Creation and inspiration, whose warm breath reminds us of summer days. Ignite our hearts with love.

 We ask for your wisdom and blessing here with us today. Please join us, Spirit of the South."

"Oh Spirit of the West, the land of the setting Sun, Of water and Autumn's whisper. Bless us with the knowledge of the peace which follows the harvest of a fruitful life. We ask for your wisdom and blessing here today. Please join us, Spirit of the West."

"Oh Spirit of the North, place of quiet, stillness, of cave and deep earth. Place of thankfulness for the knowledge and blessings that have come to us with time.

 We ask your wisdom and blessing here today. Please join us, Spirit of the North."

"Oh Spirit of Mother Earth, you support us each day, welcoming our roots deep into your heart.

You nurture and guide us finding sustenance and support. help us to give thanks Always for Your bounty.

We ask for your wisdom and blessing here today. Please join us Spirit of Mother Earth."

"Oh Spirit of Father Sky, of the angelic realms, the countless stars of the night remind us that you are vast beautiful and majestic beyond all of our knowing or understanding. Your light shines upon the earth both day and night guiding our steps.

We ask for your wisdom and blessing here today. Please join us, Father Sky."

"Oh Spirit of our souls within, Place of union, love and reverence.

We are grateful for this gift of life and for the love that guides our way.

 We open our hearts and join with all in love. It is begun."(Whispering tree.net2006-2011)

Often times we struggle within our lives.To know your our heart takes time, as well as patience.

Realize that you are made up of the same energy as the Creator.All things in this life are connected.

Sometimes ancient knowledge that you yearn to find has been with you all along.

Call upon the Ancient of Days to direct your path.Spirit like energy vibrates on a universal,scientific and spiritual level.

We too have different levels of vibration within our spirit,vibrating on the spiritual planes.

Some of us,seek beyond what we have come to know and understand.

A gift of peace washes over us,as Lady Wisdom sheds her light,where there was once a void.

Spirit is the highest level above all else,with the other elements it can not exist.Balance; essential to life which consists of,spirit,air,fire,water,and earth.

"We can apply the skills of observation and awareness,to our own patterns as well as to the patterns of nature around us.Awareness is the first step to insight,and insight is the first step to change"(The Earth Path:Grounding Your Spirit In The Rhythms Of Nature2004,Miriam Simos)

The elements can reveal many things about our daily lives,the need for change,and hope for tomorrow.

Air: encompasses our emotions,creativity,and focus.Seek deep within yourself threw meditation.

What are some of the things you can identify about your emotional life,that may be manifesting themselves within your body?

Just relax and breath in the goodness of life.Realize your blessings and be thankful for them.Release any doubt,and float as a feather.

In ancient Egyptian texts,the heart was laid upon a scale with the other end having a feather to compare it to.Strive to be free of any negative emotion that may disrupt your life.

Fire:our passion,motivation.What keeps you bound in life that you cannot create change?

The old analogy to get fired up about something makes perfect sense.Seize the day,live your life to the fullest.Create a legacy to carry on to your children.

You are a masterpiece,even if the paint brushes of life try to get you down,saying you are not worth anything.Stop repeating obsessive thoughts that keep you from accomplishing your dream!

Water: our emotions.Ask yourself what am I thirsty for?Know that you will be filled to the brim with infinite possibilities.

Drink life in,as if you were in the desert.Go with the flow life offers,although sometimes life can take us on the rapids;in the end the water becomes a peaceful stream of introspect.

Life's journey is not about the outcome,it is about experiences and lessons only learned by braving the obstacles,digging for the treasure of your own personal truths.Seeing beyond the waterfall,to find the chalice of courage.

Earth:Our bodies.Ask yourself,what have I done today to better my health?

The body is a temple and should be treated as such.At times we concentrate so much on others we have no time for ourself.

Our bodies weaken our immune system gives up the fight,we become sick.Heal yourself through taking care of your body as you would a golden treasure.

Be grounded,don't let stress overtake you!Know that the earth heals us,as we do it.A seed planted in the soil will not grow with proper care.

We too must take heed to remember to take care of our health.We come from the dust,our bodies return to it.

Our *Spirits* soar away as a released trapped bird,Our body sometimes reminds us of this,it is but a cage.A cage must have the proper framework,the bars have to be balanced and straight.We too must be balanced and grounded.

At times we entertain angels unaware,coming in all forms.Pay close attention to what your spirit is telling you,see with the eyes of your heart and keep them open.

The birds sing a secret song in our spiritual ears,the deer seeks to show us gentleness,the trees have been around for centuries their roots encompassed in mother earth,they give us oxygen;and sustane our life.The winds whisper promises of insight and wisdom.If we honor the elements of nature,the animals and the planet.

We too shall be rewarded in the end.The Prince of Peace,The Prince of the Forest,The Queen of Heaven,or the Queen of Illumination.Walk in love,and know that a label does not define our Creator,only our heart can understand the mystery.

Everyone's path is unique.There is no right or wrong one,as long as we strive to let love be our guide.

Without love,we walk blindly down the road of existence,on the road to nowhere.With faith,hope and love..a beacon of light,just past the mighty oak,illuminates our path.

The road we have traveled has been a long journey,but if not for the journey we would not have reached our destination.

We journey on,down the spiral road;that is called Self,meeting others along the way our paths seem to intertwine.The destination is the same,though many others have taken a different road all their own.The road keeps winding within itself,finally centering.

We come to a crystal clear stream at the end,peering down we see our reflection.

This is the mystery we have been seeking,Knowing ourselves journeying within to understand that we hole the key to infinity.It is found within.

We now have came to the knowledge that even though the road we take is less traveled..in the end it defines who we are,what we are here for,where we are going..and then we receive our answer of the universal question...Why?

I pray you safe journey,on your own road less traveled!Love and Light.

~~Blessed Be~~

About The Author

Marian Mayfield,resides in West Tennessee.She is a seeker of wisdom,

student of the arts of science,psychology,metaphysics and Gnosis

Her insights on belief are eclectic,she learns   lessons of life and spirituality from

many sources including nature as a whole.

In a shamanic sense,her views of the spiritual world are one of journeys of spiritual

enlightenment.Through the spiritual realm that is interconnected within all living things

she revears nature as her church.Finding Deity as an extension of all things,that radiate

with the same light of spirit.

She is well educated in theology,attending several denominations of the

Christian church throughout her life.She finds spiritual truths in the nature based

religion of Paganism ,as well as Christianity and others.

She also is a high priestess of the Lesser and Greater Eleusinian Mysteries.She wishes to

inform others who are unaware of the belief system of Paganism(An Earth Centered Religion)

of the truths behind it.That the Pagan belief being a core of nature,celebrates the life and death

and new life cycles.Just as in the story of Jesus.

.She is a mother,full time.An environmentalist,humanitarian

and a lover of all animals. Her core belief is one of love, light, and faith.

Bibliography

References and Resources

Magical Times Magazine

("The Gospel of Mary of Magdala" by Karen L. King)

("Magical Rites from the Crystal Well"Ed Fitch)

("The Natural Genesis" Gerald Massey)

Deepak Chopra

Collins English Dictionary

("Edouard Schur'e

(Ashmole's Order of the Garter")

(Manley P.Hall,"The Secret Teachings of All Ages")

"Christmas Awakening of the Heart"EdwardBach

The Irish Origins of Civilization,Micheal Tsarion

Encyclopedia Britanica

"Yggdrasil"Micheal F.Lindemans

Gospel Of Saint Thomas

"The Gospel of Mary Magdala:Jesus and the First Woman Apostle":by Karen L. King

(Whisperingtree.net2006-2011)

"(The Earth Path: Grounding Your Spirit in the Rhythms of Nature2004, Miriam Simos)

Firewytch, March 07 2007)

."(Witches, Women, and Witchcraft History and Background by Austin Cline, 2011)

Order of Bards, Ovates and Druids (OBOD)."

(Joe Panek,from the article,A Seeker's Thoughts 2010)

"History of The Kings Of Britain"1136, Geoffrey of Monmouthshire

The Gospel of Mary of Magdala: Jesus and the First Woman Apostle

by Karen L. King (Polebridge Press, Santa Rosa, California, 2003)

Mimameidr""Yggdrasil." Encyclopedia Mythica from Encyclopedia Mythica Online.

by Micha F. LindemansArticle "Yggdrasil" created on 03 March 1997)

"Celtic Myth and Magick" by Edain McCoy

"Pagans & Christians The Personal Spiritual Experience"Gus DiZerega,PH.D 2001

(The Everything Celtic Wisdom Book by:Jennifer Emick2009

(Living Gnosis A Practical Guide To Gnostic Christianity Tau Malachi 2005)

A Victorian Grimoire Enchantment Romance Magic Patricia Telesco 1998

Michael Tsarion; The Irish Origins of Civilization, Volume 1

Other Works By This Author

Jewels Of Wisdom Discovering Your Infinite Possibilities,

Jewels Of Wisdom Quest For The Crown

Made in the USA
Lexington, KY
30 May 2012